SHADOWS IN THE STRUGGLE FOR EQUALITY

The History of the Anarchist Red Cross

Boris Yelensky

Edited by Matthew Hart

Illustrated by N.O. Bonzo

PM

Shadows in the Struggle for Equality: The History of the Anarchist Red Cross
This edition © PM Press

ISBN: 979-8-88744-087-3 (paperback)
ISBN: 979-8-88744-093-4 (ebook)
LCCN: 2024939656

Cover design and art by N.O. Bonzo
Interior design by briandesign

Proceeds of this book will go to support our imprisoned comrades via the Anarchist Black Cross Federation's Warchest program.

10 9 8 7 6 5 4 3 2 1

PM Press
PO Box 23912
Oakland, CA 94623
www.pmpress.org

Printed in the USA.

CONTENTS

FOREWORD

Matthew Hart

To those reading this book for the first time, the name Boris Yelensky may not be familiar. Prior to a version of this book being published on the internet, it could be argued that the name Yelensky was truly only known to the few anarchist scholars. While during his time he was known and revered by many in the anarchist community, as generations passed on, his name, much like his decades of activism, became obscured. Most of his work, with the exception of the first printing of this book, was never published. So, unlike his more well-known compatriots, such as Emma Goldman, Peter Kropotkin, and Rudolf Rocker, the memory of Boris Yelensky faded. It is our hope that this error will soon be remedied in the pages that follow.

Boris Yelensky was born on February 17, 1889, in Krasnodar, Russia. His family eventually moved to Novorossiysk on the shores of the Black Sea. It was in Novorossiysk, a port city, that Yelensky witnessed groups of prisoners being taken off ships and loaded onto trains before being transported to far-off prisons or places of exile. The sight of worn-out groups of human beings, chained hand and foot, would have a profound impact on him in his adolescent years. At age twelve, he came upon some underground revolutionary material, and within a year he was involved in the underground revolutionary movement in the city.

When the 1905 Revolution broke out, he joined a small Socialist Revolutionaries–Maximalist group and participated in the uprising in his city. When the revolution was unsuccessful, Yelensky was forced to flee, hiding throughout the Russian territory before making it to the United States around April 1908.

Yelensky first moved to Philadelphia to stay with his cousin. Soon he joined the Radical Library, a branch of the Workmen's Circle associated with the anarchist movement. He returned to Russia in 1910 but was forced to flee back to the United States after ten months.

In 1912, Yelensky, along with Morris Beresin and Joseph Cohen, formed the Philadelphia branch of the Anarchist Red Cross (ARC). While in Philadelphia, he met and married Bessie Avedon, who was also involved in the organization. The following year the couple moved to Chicago and joined the Chicago branch of the ARC. Bessie became the secretary of the organization, which consisted of over three hundred members at the time.[1]

With news of the Russian Revolution, Boris and Bessie were among the thousands who traveled back to Russia to aid in building the new society. Boris Yelensky became active in the factory committee movement in Novorossiysk and participated in the October Revolution. He soon found himself disillusioned by the events taking place, which he has documented in his unpublished piece, "In the Social Storm."

Once they returned to the United States, the two helped to form the Russian Political Relief Committee to assist imprisoned anarchists and Social Democrats in Russia. The organization changed its name to the Chicago Aid Fund in 1925 and again in 1936 to the Alexander Berkman Aid Fund to commemorate the life of Berkman. During the Spanish Civil War, aid was extended to Spanish anarchist fugitives in several European and Latin American countries. The organization helped to publish Gregory Maximoff's *Guillotine at Work*, which reported on the Bolshevik's abuses against revolutionary movements in Russia. During this period, both Boris and Bessie were also involved in the Free Society Group of Chicago and the Workmen's Circle.

After World War II, Boris Yelensky established contact with comrades in Europe and helped to provide aid to anarchists in need throughout Europe. He continued this work until 1957 when he and Bessie retired in Florida. While in Florida, he established the Simon Farber Memorial Fund, to celebrate the life and work of a beloved comrade.

Bessie, Boris Yelensky's partner in life and in struggle, passed in June 1968. Boris would continue until his passing in June 1974. They lived their lives shaped by the principles of mutual aid, solidarity, and a determination to create a new world in the shell of the old. Yet, despite over seventy years of involvement in the anarchist movement, the names of Boris Yelensky and his life partner, Bessie, whose participation was just as significant, were nearly lost in time. There are few in the modern movement who directly connect these individuals with the contributions they made to the movement. Such a situation would probably seem apropos for Yelensky, though, as he wrote in *Shadows in the Struggle for Equality* that "the work was not done for the glory, but because we believed in Mutual Aid." It seems that he would have preferred that the work go on regardless of any credit for the work he did in the past. Perhaps that credit can be given now.

OLGA
TARATUTA

Prior to the moment this book was republished on the internet, those active in the Anarchist Black Cross (ABC) movement during the decades surrounding the beginning of the twenty-first century pointed to Lorenzo Kom'boa Ervin's *Draft Proposal for an Anarchist Black Cross Network*, originally published in 1979, as the most authoritative document concerning the movement. Despite the document being viewed as a critical text in the shaping of the movement in the coming decades, Ervin's work remained vague on the facts regarding the earliest years of the organization's existence. Like most material describing the history of the organization, Ervin wrote that the organization was born during the era of czarist Russia to aid political prisoners. It altered its name from the Anarchist Red Cross to the Anarchist Black Cross during the Russian Civil War. It fell apart in the 1930s, only to be reestablished in Britain in the 1960s. This was often the extent of historical accounts of the organization's activities. It could be argued that the early editions of the *Black Flag* publication provided much more substantial information, but old editions were not easily accessible. Ervin's proposal was republished on numerous occasions and thus became the reference point toward the building of the movement and the understanding of the organization's history.

One exception to this limitation was the work published by the anarchist historian, Paul Avrich. Avrich's *Anarchist Voices* was especially important in providing personal accounts by those active in the ABC movement in its earliest years. His research provided additional information about previously unknown chapters active prior to the Russian Revolution. Avrich did provide one simple explanation as to the reason why the earliest years of the organization were so elusive. With the exception of a few documents and

ANNA
STEPANOVA

publications, most of the material, correspondence, and firsthand documents for the ABC were written in Yiddish and Russian. Those who were searching for the past were searching in the wrong languages.

Shadows in the Struggle for Equality provides the reader with not only Yelensky's own personal account but also those of others who helped to form the organization in Russia and the United States. While it is the most comprehensive document relating to the history of the Anarchist Red Cross, there is much that has been left out. Obviously, since most of the history of the organization had yet to be established, it stands to reason that this information would not be included. However, there is much that Yelensky could have included but failed to.

One such example is the history of the Political Red Cross (or as Yelensky refers to it once: "the nonpartisan Red Cross"). The Political Red Cross was originally born out of the Narodniki movement, a nineteenth-century socialist movement that advocated spreading revolutionary propaganda to the peasants with the hope of fostering revolutionary conditions and change. The czarist repression of the Narodniki led to hundreds of political prisoners imprisoned or exiled to far-off regions of Russia. The Political Red Cross was formed to provide food, clothing, and literature, and assist in prison escapes.

In 1879, the Narodnaya Volya (People's Will) was formed, a revolutionary organization that advocated "propaganda by the deed" as a means to political change. The organization would be responsible for the assassination of several government officials including the Russian czar, Alexander II. The same year as the czar's assassination, the Red Cross Society of Narodnaya Volya was formed. To ensure its nonpartisan nature, it was led by Vera Zasulich

LIYA
GUTTMAN

and Peter Lavoff, individuals who were well respected by the various factions in the revolutionary movement.

Benjamin Tucker, a Stirnerite anarchist based in Boston, was appointed as the American agent for the Red Cross Society of Narodnaya Volya. Nikolai Tchaikovsky, who helped to ignite the Narodniki movement in Russia, became the agent in England. Peter Kropotkin, the anarchist prince and close friend of Tchaikovsky, also aided in raising funds for the organization but was critical of the Red Cross's association with Narodnaya Volya after the organization's assassination of Alexander II. He argued with Lavroff that fundraising efforts for Russian political prisoners would be undermined in the United Kingdom because of the Red Cross's association with Narodnaya Volya.

Over time, Zasulich and Lavroff struggled to keep the organization separate from Narodnaya Volya, which regularly attempted to wield greater control over the Red Cross and its finances. This eventually led to the resignation of Zasulich from the organization entirely. With Zasulich's absence and members of Narodnaya Volya and the Political Red Cross facing arrests and imprisonment because of their illegal status, the organization grew increasingly ineffective. Within a few short years, the People's Will was dissolved. Soon the Russian Social Democratic Labor Party would emerge, and it too attempted to shape the disbursement of resources within the Political Red Cross. The Russian Social Democratic Labor Party's attempt to redirect funds to prisoners of their own political persuasion was what eventually led to the establishment of the Anarchist Red Cross. This new organization would ensure that anarchists took it upon themselves to support their comrades in Russian prisons or in exile.

Another subject omitted from Yelensky's book was the various informants who infiltrated the Anarchist Red Cross, particularly the Chicago chapter. This may not have been intentional but rather because Yelensky was unaware of the informants at the time. One alleged informant of the Chicago Anarchist Red Cross was Morris Bernstein.[2] Bernstein was involved in a curious incident in January 1914, in which he and several others were arrested during an unemployment protest. An anonymous letter was sent to the police station threatening to blow up the building if he was not released. The threat was followed with another, this time written on the door of an employer's home stating that if he did not pay a hundred dollars, he and his wife would be harmed. Both threats came with a drawing of a skull and cross bones and were written in red. The press and police attributed these incidents to the Anarchist Red Cross despite having no evidence.[3]

Six years later, as part the continued nationwide raids against radicals, Bernstein's bookstore was raided, and a large cache of communist and anarchist material was seized. It was at this time that Bernstein's role as an informant was revealed by the Chicago police to the federal authorities. The Chicago police indicated that Bernstein had recently become an informant and had provided valuable information to the authorities.[4]

The Chicago Anarchist Red Cross was also infiltrated by Albert Bailin (believed to be an alias used by Albert Balanow). Bailin was hired by various detective agencies to spy on anarchist and communist organizations. In May 1917, Bailin was arrested with Max Lurye and Jacob Billow for the distribution of anarchist literature. All men were described as members of the Anarchist Red Cross, although it was later discovered that Billow was also acting on behalf of the Chicago police and employers to monitor and disrupt the Cigar Makers' Union.[5]

After the Wall Street bombing in September 1920, letters were sent to the postmaster in New York stating that the Woolworth Building would be destroyed if political prisoners were not released. It was signed by the "Knights of the Red Star," an alleged anarchist organization. Bailin indicated that he had intimate knowledge of the organization, but it was later revealed that Bailin had been responsible for the threat in hopes of continuing his employment as an informant for the federal government.[6] It is not unreasonable to suggest that Bailin's inspiration for the name came from the Anarchist Red Cross.

The continued monitoring and harassment of the Anarchist Red Cross led to raids, arrests, and even deportation. Jacob Goodman of the Chicago chapter was arrested for his involvement in the Anarchist Red Cross and the Chicago chapter of the Milwaukee Defense League.[7] Morris Schnitman and Esther Berman of the New York chapter were arrested in Colorado and were suspected of traveling to Mexico to contact Emiliano Zapata.[8] Morris Waisman of the Milwaukee chapter had his home and workplace raided, and Anarchist Red Cross material was seized. All these individuals were slated to be deported for their political activities and association with the Anarchist Red Cross.[9] However, the deportation orders were eventually dismissed. Not everyone was so lucky. Hyman Perkus of the Cleveland Anarchist Red Cross was deported to Russia, along with his partner, Dora Lipkin, for involvement in the Union of Russian Workers.[10]

Yelensky's failure to mention these incidents may be a simple oversight or may be attributed to the fact that the mass arrests and deportations of anarchists, communists, and socialists overshadowed the few arrests related to Anarchist Red Cross activities. One could argue that the targeting of groups like the Union of Russian Workers by the federal government makes the harassment against the Anarchist Red Cross seem miniscule at best. But in examining the history of the Anarchist Red Cross, it is important to recognize the targeting of the organization in its early years, especially since this would certainly become a greater concern for those active in the organization subsequently.

One significant matter that was overlooked in Yelensky's *Shadows in the Struggle for Equality* was the Latvian section of the Anarchist Red Cross and its connection to the Lexington Avenue explosion on July 4, 1914. The explosion left four dead, including two members of the organization, Charles Berg and Carl Hanson. The apartment where the incident took place was rented by Louise Berger, another member of the organization. In order to ensure that the history of that event is included, an addendum has been included in this edition of the book.

While many revolutionaries, like Yelensky, traveled to Russia after the Revolution broke out in 1917, it soon became clear that the hope of a new society would not come to fruition. Again, there became a need for the Anarchist Red Cross (now renamed the Anarchist Black Cross) to be reestablished. The organization was quickly criminalized in the Soviet Union. It is for this reason that the organization also used the name Moscow Society to Aid Imprisoned Anarchists. But regardless of the banner the organization worked under, members of the Anarchist Black Cross repeatedly found themselves under arrest because of their aid to political prisoners and for communicating with the outside world about the abuses that were going on within the prison walls of the Bolshevik government.

Tatyana Polosova, a member of the Moscow Society to Aid Imprisoned Anarchists, was arrested while she attempted to bring a child to visit their imprisoned anarchist parent. Molly Steimer, an anarchist who had been deported from the United States, was arrested for aiding imprisoned anarchists and corresponding with her comrades abroad. Lea Gutman and Helena Ganshina, also delegates for the aid organization, were sent to travel to the north to distribute food, clothing, and other vital necessities among the political prisoners in the prisons and camps of Archangel Province. During their trip, the anarchists in Pertominsky Prison declared a hunger strike for better living conditions. Because Gutman, Ganshina, and another comrade informed the others in Petrograd and Moscow about the hunger strike, they were arrested and sent to a Moscow prison. Both Gutman and Ganshina were sentenced to two years in Berezov in Siberia. A seven-day hunger strike forced the authorities to change the place of exile. Gutman was transferred and remained in exile in the town of Zinovievsk. Ganshina was transferred from prison to prison and was last known to have been in Siberia.

Olga Taratuta and Anna Ivanovna Stepanova were founding members of the Anarchist Black Cross in Ukraine. The Ukraine section was unique in that it also organized self-defense and medical units during conflicts with the counterrevolutionary armies during the civil war that followed the Revolution. During combat, members would distinguish themselves by wearing overalls and armbands. The Anarchist Black Cross worked closely with the Nabat Confederation, an anarchist organization in Ukraine, as well Makhno's army, an anarchist insurgent army that was critical in pushing back the counterrevolutionary forces in Ukraine. Despite the Nabat Confederation and

BESSIE YELENSKY

Makhno's army playing critical roles in the defeat of counterrevolutionary forces in the region, in November 1920, the Bolshevik government raided Makhno's headquarters and arrested numerous leaders of the Nabat Confederation, including Olga Taratuta.[11] Stepanova was also soon arrested. The office of the Anarchist Black Cross was destroyed by the Bolshevik government as part of the raids.

The Anarchist Black Cross continued to function within Russia for many years despite its illegal status. By 1925, many of its members had been arrested, and prisoner support became more of a clandestine activity. Other organizations, such as the Bureau of Anarchists for the Protection of Sacco and Vanzetti formed in Russia to shed light on the incarceration of the two anarchists in the United States, but members also found themselves arrested when they raised criticism of the repressive conduct of the Bolshevik government against anarchists in Russia.[12]

Those who had participated in the Anarchist Red Cross prior to the Revolution also found themselves the targets of Bolshevik repression. Efim Yarchuk of the New York Anarchist Red Cross helped lead the Kronstadt sailors during the October Revolution. However, his dedication to his anarchist ideals would lead to numerous arrests at the hands of the Bolsheviks. He participated in the 1921 Taganka Prison strike, which led to his deportation from Russia. Alexander Schapiro, who had acted as the secretary of the London Anarchist Red Cross before returning to Russia, was arrested by the Bolshevik government for allegedly working with the underground anarchist movement. He was eventually exiled to Berlin. There he joined the Joint Committee for the Defense of the Revolutionaries Imprisoned in Russia with Gregory Maximoff, Alexander Berkman, and Emma Goldman.

LOUISE BERGER

In January 1921, Alexander Berkman, Alexander Schapiro, and Emma Goldman made an appeal to the world to aid those comrades who were suffering under the Bolshevik regime. The international anarchist community came together to support Russian prisoners. In 1922, the International Aid Federation formed to help anarchists in Russia and Spain. The following year, the Group for the Relief of Russian Anarchists published *Hilsruf,* a Yiddish newspaper with contributions from Berkman, Rudolf Rocker, and others. The group quickly reestablished itself as the London Anarchist Red Cross. In May 1923, it was announced in *Freedom*, a London-based anarchist newspaper, that the Anarchist Red Cross had reformed in New York. Other groups formed in France, Germany, and Argentina with the purpose of providing aid.[13]

In September 1923, an article was published in *Freedom* that called for all workers to condemn the Russian government for its abuses and to support those imprisoned by the regime. Out of this call, the Joint Committee for the Defense of the Revolutionaries Imprisoned in Russia began to publish a bulletin with the names and stories of those who were imprisoned or in exile in Russia. The publication would eventually turn into the *Bulletin of the Relief Fund of International Working Men's Association for Anarchists and Anarcho-Syndicalists Imprisoned or Exiled in Russia.*

The bulletin continued to be published into the 1930s and provided some details that may contradict some information provided in this book. Yelensky claimed the Anarchist Red Cross in New York disbanded in 1926, leaving Chicago to be the only group working regularly for the aid of anarchist prisoners. There is no doubt that he is only addressing organizations in the United States and not globally since the London Anarchist Red Cross and the

JACQUES
DOUBINSKY

International Working Men's Association (IWMA) were still collecting funds for anarchists in Russia. But even if that were the case, the New York Anarchist Red Cross was still providing funds to the IWMA well into 1928. The Los Angeles Aid Society for Political Prisoners was in existence for several years with Arestantin Balls being organized in Los Angeles as late as 1932. While it is true that the Berkman Aid Fund was the most effective in raising funds for Russian anarchist prisoners, other organizations still worked to raise funds for imprisoned comrades, whether that was solely or just part of their mission.

While anarchists still continued to provide support, a greater concern was revealing itself in Russia. Although many anarchists were deported and escaped from the Soviet Union, there were those who remained, either continuing their anarchist activities or joining the Bolshevik Party. Some, like Efim Yarchuk, returned to Russia after leaving or being exiled. Unfortunately, their ties to the anarchist cause, regardless of whether their convictions remained or changed, would continue to haunt them and, for many, caused them to fall victim to the purges under Stalin. Several members of the Anarchist Red Cross were among those individuals affected. Yarchuk was arrested and executed in 1937. William Shatoff, a former member of the Anarchist Red Cross in New York who tried to work with the Bolshevik Party, was arrested in December 1936 and eventually killed by a firing squad. Hyman Perkus, who worked with the Cleveland and New York Anarchist Red Cross, was also reported to have been killed during the purges, but details regarding his death are scant. After repeated arrests for her anarchist activities, Olga Taratuta was rearrested in November 1937 and charged with being an anarchist and engaging in anti-Soviet activity. On

February 8, 1938, she was condemned to death by the Chief Tribunal of the Soviet Union and was executed the same day. Another member of the Anarchist Black Cross, Ivan Kharkhardin, was continuously harassed for his participation in various anarchist organizations until his arrest in 1939 when he was sentenced to ten years in a prison camp. He was never heard from again.

The repressive measures and the disappearance of anarchists during the Stalinist purges made it impossible for the anarchist prisoner aid community outside of Russia to continue providing support to those in the country. With the exception of support for imprisoned anarchists, like Ricardo Flores Magón, the sole purpose for the Anarchist Red Cross was to aid those imprisoned in Russia. This caused debate as to whether the organization had served its purpose.

However, the political conditions in Europe soon illustrated that the need for anarchist aid organizations was as great as ever. But the aid that was needed was less about supporting those imprisoned and more about helping those trying to escape a worse kind of fate. With the rise of fascism that infected Europe beginning in the 1930s, a new level of inhumanity surfaced. The Spanish Civil War and the rise of the Franco government created a mass exodus of exiled Spanish republicans and anarchists into France, Mexico, and South America. Those who fled to France and other regions in Europe soon themselves fleeing from the encroaching Nazi military. The Nazis were engaging in mass imprisonment of political and ethnic undesirables, and in mass genocide and murder of those seen as inferior to the Aryan race. Anarchists, many of whom escaped the oppressive Bolshevik regime in Russia, now needed to find the means of escaping the rise of fascism and all the brutality that came with it. This was certainly the situation for those comrades of Jewish ethnicity, who would certainly find themselves in death camps. Most had little resources to escape to a safe location or found it difficult to get the visas necessary to escape.

The Alexander Berkman Aid Fund and other organizations began to shift their resources to assist anarchists who were attempting to escape from Europe. Yelensky has provided a great deal of information in this book concerning the Alexander Berkman Aid Fund and other organizations' roles in providing aid and how political friction with Marxist-leaning organizations interfered with supplying those resources. However, it seems that political factionalism in the anarchist movement also played a role in how resources were distributed throughout Europe once the war was over.

After the end of World War II, the Alexander Berkman Aid Fund (ABAF), along with Sveriges Abetares Centralorganisation (SAC, Swedish Central Workers' Organization), the International Anti-Fascist Solidarity (SIA) in Paris, and the International Anarchist Solidarity (SAI) in Argentina mobilized to aid anarchists imprisoned in Spain, as well as those in exile. The ABAF established a section in Paris under the direction of Jacques Doubinsky, a Jewish Ukrainian anarchist who fought with the Makhnovist movement before settling in Paris. The ABAF in Chicago, with help from anarchist organizations in New York, Detroit, and Los Angeles, collected funds, food, clothing, and medicine. Packages were sent through CARE (Cooperative for American Remittances to Europe), created in 1945 to organize the delivery of aid to postwar Europe.

In its efforts to provide solidarity and support to comrades abroad, the ABAF found itself caught in a political divide between two political factions within the Spanish anarchist movement. The conflict divided the Confederación Nacional del Trabajo (CNT, or National Confederation of Labor) into a political wing and an apolitical wing. The political wing, which was represented by the "Interior" CNT, was in favor of collaborating with the exiled republican government and socialists. This faction was prevalent inside Spain, apart from the Spanish anarchist youth who took a more militant stance. The apolitical wing, represented by the MLE-CNT (Spanish Libertarian Movement-CNT), rejected coalitions with other anti-Franco movements and placed an emphasis on armed struggle. This faction was predominant outside of Spain and attracted the anarchist youth organizations, such as Juventudes Libertarias (Libertarian Youth). The split was exacerbated by financial discrepancies that were left unanswered by the MLE-CNT. Harsh criticism by the members of the "Interior" CNT led to their expulsion from the organization.[14]

At first the conflict between the two factions did not interfere with the work of the ABAF. Due to the Franco government's strict policies, the ABAF could not send funds directly to anarchists held in Spanish prisons. Attempts to do so could cause them serious harm. As such, the ABAF sent funds to groups representing both factions outside of Spain, who would then use their contacts to ensure the funds got sent to the families of prisoners and then to the prisoners themselves. For Yelensky, this arrangement was not ideal since the ABAF was generally able to find the means to communicate and verify that the aid was received; but attempts to renegotiate the terms were often met with the potential reality of putting the anarchist prisoners or their families in harm's way.

Yelensky caused further annoyance when he communicated with both factions that he wanted to ensure that the funds being sent were used only to support anarchist prisoners and not for organizational purposes. Yelensky attempted to make clear that the ABAF did not want to get involved in the factional struggles but just wanted the money to go to the libertarian prisoners in Franco's prisons. He argued that the ABAF did not care on which side of the feud they fell, the ABAF simply did not want the funds to be used for fights between bosses and bosses, for factionalist propaganda, or things like that. The money was collected for libertarian prisoners, and this should be its destination. This seemed to offend representatives of the MLE-CNT, who claimed that the directive left them feeling mistreated.[15]

Despite wishing to remain neutral, the ABAF started to send funds only to the "Internal" CNT, beginning in 1954. This was allegedly because the MLE-CNT stopped communicating with the Berkman Aid Fund. The "Internal" CNT continued to request funds, so the funds were diverted to them. However, in early 1956, Yelensky learned from the ABAF's section in Paris that a representative from the International Anti-Fascist Solidarity (SIA) had been stating to anarchists in New York that the Alexander Berkman Aid Fund had only been providing aid to minority groups in opposition to the larger Spanish anarchist movement.

Yelensky attempted to resolve the situation by writing to both the MLE-CNT and the "Internal" CNT, stating:

> The Alexander Berkman Aid Fund and in the previous years the Anarchist Red Cross, never took any part in the internal fights in our movements . . . and I want to add that in the half of a century that I am

MOLLIE STEIMER

active in this work, we never were accused that our
organization is unfair to one or another grouping in
our movement.... Last year we received news from
New York, that some of the Spanish Comrades are
accusing the A. Berkman Fund in unfairness toward
the Anarchists in Spain, because we sent the money
on the above address [47, rue Jonquieres, Toulouse].
It is very unpleasant situation for us, that after so
many years of work that we should be accused to
be unfair.[16]

Despite attempts to resolve the matter, a representative from the MLE-CNT remained unwavering in the
criticism of the ABAF and their lack of understanding of
the dynamics within the Spanish anarchist movement.[17]

To add to Yelensky's frustration, he was informed
several months later that the ABAF decided to continue
to send funds solely to the "Internal" CNT. Boris and Bessie
had moved to Miami and were no longer involved in the
day-to-day activities of the organization. Further investigation into the matter led Yelensky to conclude that he
and other members of the organization were not given the
full information by Martin Gudell, another member of the
ABAF and the only member of the organization that spoke
Spanish. Outraged, Yelensky broke all ties with the ABAF
after forty years of providing support to imprisoned anarchist comrades.[18]

Despite leaving the organization, Yelensky felt that his
reputation and the reputation of the ABAF had been put
into question. In all the years of advocating for anarchist
prisoners, neither he nor the fund had ever been accused
of taking sides in a factional dispute within the anarchist
movement. In an attempt to resolve the matter, a portion of

SENYA FLESHIN

the proceeds of *In the Struggle for Equality* were sent to the MLE-CNT. Shortly after Yelensky's exit from the organization, the ABAF ceased its activities sometime around 1958.

For a time, the Anarchist Red Cross / Anarchist Black Cross would remain defunct. It seemed that Yelensky would be the last word on the history of the organization. Unbeknownst to him it would soon be revived, and a movement that seemed to be slowly dying out over decades would be revitalized and continue to grow stronger. The organization would also find itself interwoven with a new generation of anarchists determined to change the world around them by any means necessary. Yelensky's *In the Struggle for Equality* would not be the final pages written on the Anarchist Black Cross.

THE SECOND WAVE

The rebirth of the Anarchist Black Cross began with two men, Albert Meltzer and Stuart Christie. Meltzer was a London-based anarchist who had been active in the movement since the age of fifteen. He quickly drew attention to himself by contradicting Emma Goldman at a meeting over her criticism of boxing. Meltzer built a reputation as a militant anarchist and trade unionist. During the Battle of Cable Street in October 1936, Meltzer was among those who fought Mosley's Blackshirts. During the Spanish Civil War, he assisted in smuggling guns to those fighting against Franco's regime. In 1946, he took part in the Cairo Mutiny after being conscripted into the British Army.

Stuart Christie was a Glasgow-born anarchist, who joined the nuclear disarmament movement at age sixteen. In 1964, Christie made contact with the Federación Ibérica de Juventudes Libertarias (FIJL, the Iberian Federation of Libertarian Youth) in the hope of joining the anti-Franco resistance movement. He was quickly introduced to militants with the Defensa Interior (DI), an organization that united the FIJL, MLE-CNT, and the FAI (Iberian Anarchist Federation) under one umbrella with the purpose of planning clandestine activities. Unfortunately for Christie, the police forces in the United Kingdom and Spain coordinated with one another to monitor the revolutionary movements growing across Europe. Christie was arrested in Madrid on August 11, 1964, in possession of an explosive to be used in a plot to assassinate Franco. He was sentenced to twenty years in prison. However, due to an international campaign, Christie was released from prison in September 1967.

Albert Meltzer and Stuart Christie had been corresponding while Christie languished in the Spanish prison. After Christie was released, Meltzer offered him a job at the Wooden Shoe bookstore in London. They revived the Anarchist Black Cross in the autumn of 1967 in order to provide support for the Spanish political prisoners that organizations like Amnesty International refused to support.

During the 1968 International Anarchist Conference in Carrara, Italy, the emerging generation of anarchists discussed the idea of relaunching the Anarchist Black Cross as an international prisoner support organization. The original idea was to establish the organization to aid Spanish anarchist political prisoners, but with the rise of revolutionary movements and the repression that followed, the organization took on a broader role coordinating protests, conducting or organizing agitational actions, countering state repression, and providing support to anarchist prisoners throughout the world.[19] The organization would also occupy an interesting space between aboveground and underground communities. Members of the organization would often find themselves either participating in both spaces or being accused of doing so. This would lead to several significant incidents and court cases that would shape the movement and, to some degree, history.

One such example is that of the Milan chapter of the Anarchist Black Cross. After returning home from the conference in Carrara, several Milanese anarchists, Umberto del Grande, Amedeo Bertolo, and Giuseppe Pinelli formed the Milan Anarchist Black Cross in March 1969. Beyond providing support to anarchist prisoners, the group also monitored neofascist activities in Italy and Greece. They discovered that the neofascist movements were preparing for a right-wing junta to take over Italy, similar to what had been done in Greece. In what became known as the "strategy of tension," the neofascists were engaging in a series of bombings throughout Italy that were incorrectly being tied to the anarchist movement. By December 1969, over four hundred neofascist bombing incidents were falsely attributed to anarchists.[20]

In early December 1969, during the trial of six anarchists accused of a Milan bombing, Giuseppe Pinelli was able to provide the court with a dossier published by the *Observer* providing evidence of the plot, but the magistrate refused to admit it into evidence.[21]

On December 12, 1969, four bombs exploded in Rome and Milan. One bomb in Piazza Fontana in Milan killed sixteen people and wounded a hundred more. Over one hundred anarchists were arrested over the next twenty-four hours, including several members of the Milan Anarchist Black Cross. Pinelli was one of those detained.[22]

Pinelli was held for over forty-eight hours in police custody where he was beaten and interrogated. In the late hours of December 15, just around midnight, Pinelli's body was seen falling from the fourth floor. Police originally claimed that he had jumped after he admitted to the bombings, although an autopsy showed he was either dead or unconscious before he hit the ground. Despite an investigation, no one was charged with Pinelli's death.[23]

Anarchist Black Cross chapters in Germany also found themselves in conflict with police. By 1971, several Anarchist Black Cross and Black Aid organizations formed throughout Germany, including in Cologne, Berlin, Hannover, Norden, and Heidelberg. They organized to support the Spanish anarchist prisoners and those incarcerated by the ever-increasing repressive measures by the West German state. However, they themselves quickly fell under the investigation of the police.[24]

In February 1972, after the anarchist newspaper *Befreiung* (Liberation) printed a cartoon of a pig dressed in the German national colors and a swastika, police raided their office, which they shared with the Cologne Black Cross. The police arrested members of both the *Befreiung* and Anarchist Black Cross and seized the funds of the Black Cross. They were accused of inciting hatred, defamation of the Federal Republic of Germany, and supporting the Baader-Meinhof group, an underground guerilla group active in Germany. The evidence regarding the support of the Baader-Meinhof group was rooted in the fact that the Cologne Black Cross was supporting imprisoned members of the organization.[25]

Three years later, on April 14, 1975, a member of the Cologne Black Cross, Ralf Stein, was arrested by the "anti-terror squad" and charged with criminal association, illegal possession of guns and ammunition, helping an escaped prisoner, and several other charges. He was sentenced to eighteen months in prison. The state argued that Stein, as a member of both the *Befreiung* and the Black

Cross, sympathized with terrorists since the Black Cross supported political prisoners that had engaged in guerilla campaigns. The state also claimed that he was connected to a group that was hiding guns for terrorist groups. Stein denied any involvement in such acts but was still sentenced to eighteen months in prison.[26]

While Stein denied any involvement in underground activities, several members of the Berlin Black Cross blurred the line of legal and extralegal activity, if not crossed it completely. Georg von Rauch, Thomas Weissbecker, and Michael "Bommi" Baumann had been living together in Wieland Commune when they formed the Hash Rebels. The group organized various acts of protests including smoke-ins but soon began to escalate their tactics. After traveling to Jordan to receive training in underground tactics and strategies, they formed the Tupamaros West-Berlin. The group engaged in a series of attacks in support of anti-imperialist struggles throughout the world. Despite their involvement in underground activities, the three men remained active in the Anarchist Black Cross, with von Rauch acting as its secretary.[27]

By July 1971, the three men found themselves in court, charged with a 1970 assault on a right-wing journalist. Weissbecker and Baumann were found not guilty, but this was not the case for Georg von Rauch, who was facing ten years in prison. Due to their similar appearance, the media, police, and court officials often confused Weissbecker and von Rauch, so when the sentencing was handed down, the two anarchists switched roles, allowing the police to mistakenly take Weissbecker into custody. Weissbecker wittingly chose not to reveal the error until von Rauch had escaped. Once Weissbecker disclosed his identity, he was released from custody.[28]

ALBERT MELTZER

After the court hearing, all three went underground, where they formed the June 2nd Movement. The organization derived its name from the date when a university student, Benno Ohnesorg, was killed while participating in a protest. However, life underground was short-lived when on December 4, 1971, Georg von Rauch and several others were pulled over by police. It remains unclear who opened fire first, but a shootout between the police and those pulled over left Georg von Rauch dead. Michael "Bommi" Baumann, who was present during the incident, managed to escape.[29] Three months later, on March 2, 1972, Thomas Weissbecker was killed during a shootout with Munich police. Baumann was eventually arrested in a squat in London in February 1981. He was deported to Germany where he was sentenced to a five-year, two-month sentence for two bank robberies and a bombing of a Berlin police station. It was later reported that while underground, he was arrested by the East German Stasi in 1972. During that time, he provided information about numerous people in the armed struggle movement in West Germany. After this was revealed in 1998, Baumann was shunned by former comrades as a police informer.[30]

Another chapter whose activities transitioned into the extralegal was the Dublin Anarchist Black Cross. The anarchist movement does not have deep roots in Ireland. The political landscape has always been shaped by the Irish republican struggle against English occupation. However, by the 1960s, inflamed by the global struggles against imperialism and the civil rights movement taking place in the north, an anarchist community began to develop in Dublin. Groups, like the Dublin Anarchist Group and the New Earth group, quickly made their presence known in the community through aggressive

STUART CHRISTIE

demonstrations but would soon transition to more militant forms of actions.

The Dublin Anarchist Black Cross was formed in the later months of 1968 and had a shared membership with some of the other organizations.[31] Noel and Marie Murray, for example, helped to form the Dublin Anarchist Black Cross but were active in the New Earth group, another local anarchist group. In March and April of 1974, five members of the New Earth group were arrested, along with two other anarchists. Charges included possession of firearms and explosives, armed robbery, and participation in attacks on Iberia Airlines, the Spanish Cultural Institute, and financial institutions. All the men received various sentences. Marie Murray received a two-year suspended sentence. Noel Murray went underground to avoid prison. Marie soon joined him.[32]

On September 12, 1975, an off-duty police officer was killed during a bank robbery in Dublin. One month later Noel and Marie Murray, along with Ronan Stenson, were arrested and charged with killing the police officer. All three confessed after several days of extensive interrogation and torture.[33]

The three were tried with the Murrays being found guilty and sentenced to be hanged. Stenson's case was dismissed because it was declared that he was unlawfully detained. Due to international pressure, the Supreme Court in Ireland substituted the verdict, with Noel Murray being given a life sentence and a new trial was ordered for Marie Murray. She too was eventually given a life sentence. In 1992, the two were released from prison.[34]

Those associated with the London Anarchist Black Cross faced a considerable amount of suspicion and allegations by numerous governments across Europe for

IRIS MILLS

alleged involvement or association with the underground anarchist/anti-Franco movement. While the degree of participation will likely never be known, it cannot be denied that the allegations made against the organization had some merit. *Black Flag*, the anarchist publication produced by the London Anarchist Black Cross, certainly became a mouthpiece for the International Revolutionary Solidarity Movement, a network of underground groups consisting of the First of May, the Angry Brigade, and other like-minded underground organizations.

Because of Stuart Christie's imprisonment for the attempted assassination of Franco, police were certain that any action by anarchist/anti-Franco guerilla organizations on English soil were connected in some way to him. However, the First of May Group, an anti-Franco anarchist revolutionary organization, was already engaging in a campaign in the UK before Christie was even released from Spanish prison. In April 1967, the First of May Group kidnapped the Spanish ambassador's personal secretary and the legal attaché of the Spanish embassy. Both were later released. In August, the group used a machine gun to attack two cars owned by Spanish diplomats and the US embassy.[35]

After Christie's release, he was regularly questioned about his connection to the ongoing First of May Group attacks. In March 1969, Alan Barlow and Phil Carver, two anarchists who lived in the flat below Christie, were arrested in connection to a First of May Group bombing of Banco de Bilbao in the Covent Garden area of London. Barlow eventually pled guilty to the attack and received a twelve-month sentence. Carver was given a twelve-month suspended sentenced. Police would later claim that the bombing of Banco de Bilbao was not the act of the First of May Group but was committed by the Angry Brigade.[36]

The first alleged action by the Angry Brigade was on May 22, 1970; it targeted the police station in Paddington, an area in central London. On January 12, 1971, the Angry Brigade set off several bombs targeting the home of Robert Carr, the secretary of state for employment.[37] The media reported that police wanted to arrest a specific anarchist who was suspected in the previous bombings. Clearly Christie was the person under suspicion. Police had already engaged in a series of unsuccessful raids at Christie's home in search of explosives.[38]

In response to the Carr bombing, raids significantly increased. Police arrested Jake Prescott and Ian Purdie for alleged involvement in the Angry Brigade actions. Prescott would eventually be sentenced to fifteen years in prison; Purdie was acquitted due to lack of evidence. On August 20, 1971, police raided a home and arrested Jim Greenfield, Anna Mendelssohn, John Barker, and Hilary Creek. The next day Christopher Bott and Stuart Christie were arrested when they came to visit the home unaware that a raid had taken place the previous day. Several other anarchists were also arrested, but only two others, Angela Weir and Kate McLean, were charged. The group would become known as the Stoke Newington Eight.[39]

The trial lasted just over six months. Jim Greenfield, Anna Mendelssohn, John Barker, and Hilary Creek were all found guilty of conspiring to cause explosions. The remaining four (Christopher Bott, Angela Weir, Kate McLean, and Stuart Christie) were acquitted on all charges. The case against Christie was based on circumstantial evidence and detonators that had been planted in his car. Those who were found guilty were sentenced to ten years.[40]

The government's theory was that the Angry Brigade was the British section of the First of May Group, and that Christie was their facilitator. And to some degree, the London Anarchist Black Cross did play a role in bringing the various factions together. The group acted as a hub where generations of anarchists and revolutionaries came together to share ideas, theories, and strategies for changing society in a fundamental way. In many ways, it helped the older generation pass the baton to the next generation.

When the Spanish anarchist Miguel García was released from Spanish prison in October 1969 after twenty years, Christie persuaded García to move to London and act as the international secretary of the Anarchist Black Cross. Miguel García and Albert Meltzer established the Centro Ibérico / International Libertarian Centre, which was often visited by members of the Movimiento Ibérico de Liberación (MIL), an anti-Franco guerilla group active throughout Europe. Several members of the MIL were described by Stuart Christie as being activists involved in the Centro Ibérico and the Anarchist Black Cross.

Oriol Solé Sugranyes and another MIL member were arrested on September 16, 1973, while trying to cross the border from Spain to France. He was shot trying to escape from prison in April 1973. Eight days after Sugranyes's arrest, three more MIL members were arrested in a police ambush in Barcelona.[41] One of the three, Salvador Puig Antich, like Sugranyes, had been active with the Centro Ibérico and the Anarchist Black Cross during his time in London. During the ambush, a member of Franco's secret police, Brigada Politico Social, was killed. Although the autopsy revealed he may have been killed by his own colleague's bullets, the MIL members were sentenced to death. Puig Antich was ordered to die by garrote, an iron collar which is slowly tightened around the victim's neck

until they are strangled. Despite international protest, the Spanish government executed Antich on March 2, 1974.[42]

On May 9, 1976, two members of the Groupes d'Action Révolutionnaires Internationalistes (GARI), Robert Touati and Juan Duran Escribano, were killed when a bomb they were carrying exploded prematurely on the campus of the Toulouse-Rangueil University. The GARI was formed after the death of Puig Antich and the crackdown on the MIL. Both men, Touati and Duran Escribano, were associated with the Centro Iberico / Anarchist Black Cross Centre.[43]

In May 1977, six individuals, including several members of the Anarchist Black Cross in Huddersfield, UK, were arrested and charged with conspiracy to cause explosions to persons unknown. This case became known as the "Person Unknown" trial. Much like the Angry Brigade trial, the case brought the Anarchist Black Cross into the national headlines. Iris Mills and Ronan Bennett were active in the Anarchist Black Cross and the case's main defendants. Mills had come from Australia with her partner, Graham Rua. The two joined the Anarchist Black Cross / *Black Flag* group in London before moving to Huddersfield and starting an affinity group there. Ronan Bennett had been imprisoned for his involvement in the Irish republican movement and had been corresponding with the Anarchist Black Cross. Once released, he joined Mills and Rua in Huddersfield.[44]

Throughout the trial, the state attempted to paint the six as hardened revolutionaries who robbed supermarkets in order to fund a bombing campaign targeting government institutions. The state's case was emboldened by one defendant's admission of his involvement in robberies. In the end, the jury did not believe that the government proved their case, and four were found not guilty. Stewart

NOEL MURRAY

Carr, the defendant who admitted to the robbery charges, was the only one sentenced.[45] The sixth defendant, Dafydd Ladd, skipped bail and went underground but was later arrested for an alleged bombing campaign by the so-called Workers' Army of the Welsh Republic.

In October 1977, three individuals involved in the London Anarchist Black Cross, Dave Campbell, Brian Gibbons, and Phil Ruff, robbed a betting shop in Lewisham. However, the men were arrested as they exited after police were tipped off by an employee who thought they looked suspicious. The three were sentenced to seven years in prison.[46] Ruff, who was the cartoonist for *Black Flag*, was sent to Gartree Prison, where a riot broke out in October 1978. Ruff was singled out in the subsequent investigation because of his anarchist beliefs. He was placed in solitary confinement to restrict his access to other prisoners and ensure his anarchistic views did not spread. Throughout the Persons Unknown case, the state worked tirelessly to connect that case to the Lewisham Three. While there was a connection through Anarchist Black Cross / *Black Flag*, there was no evidence of a mass conspiracy.[47]

After the Angry Brigade trial, Stuart Christie and his wife and fellow Anarchist Black Cross member, Brenda, moved to Honley, England. This was prompted after the kidnapping in Paris of a Francoist banker, when a special branch officer advised Christie to leave London for his own safety. The couple eventually moved to the Orkney Islands, where they continued their political activity. With the move from London and the death of Franco in 1975, it would be safe to assume that the connection to the anti-Franco underground movement would die with the dictator. However, a reminder that the past is not far behind came in May 1981 when Brenda Christie was arrested while traveling in West Berlin for her alleged involvement in a First of May attack at the Frankfurt airport in May 1970. The West German government claimed that she was the individual that called to purchase the ticket for the individual that allegedly planted the bomb. International protests pressured the West German government to release her, which they finally did, without charges, more than a week after her arrest.[48]

While the Anarchist Black Cross in England, Ireland, Italy, and Germany seemed to be defined by tragedy, prosecution, and peripheral or direct involvement with the various aspects of the underground movement, other chapters throughout the world did not follow the same path as those in Europe.

The Chicago Anarchist Black Cross, for example, was formed in March 1972, after a visit from Graham Rua of the London and later Huddersfield Anarchist Black Cross. The Chicago group worked out of the Solidarity Bookshop, run by the Industrial Workers of the World. The chapter started by providing support for Spanish and Italian anarchists but expanded their work to include Western Hemisphere prisoners. The Chicago group also published the *ABC Bulletin*, taking inspiration from the *Black Flag* publication in London. The bulletin was published from July 1972 to January 1974. The group's activities seemed short-lived and there is no account of the group after 1974.[49]

The Melbourne Anarchist Black Cross was formed in 1973 by several Spanish anarchists in exile. They formed to provide support to anarchists imprisoned in Spain and to provide aid to the anti-Franco resistance. The group published the journal *Acracia*, which was originally in Spanish, but was soon converted into a bilingual publication after former students from three universities in Melbourne joined the organization. The group also spread its activities to Sydney. The group continued for several years and then disbanded following the death of Franco.

Chapters in Seattle, Denmark, Tokyo, and Brussels are reported to have been formed according to the *Black Flag* publication, but there is little reporting of their activities after their existence was announced.

THIRD WAVE

In 1979, Lorenzo Kom'boa Ervin, an anarchist political prisoner in the US, issued a *Draft Proposal for an ABC Network* in hopes that it could build a more comprehensive movement to assist anarchist political prisoners. He believed that the Anarchist Black Cross should be a united mass movement rather than individual collectives. While most of the chapters of the previous decade seemed to fade away, the London group continued to publish *Black Flag,* helping to spread the information about continuing movements and the need for support for those anarchists imprisoned in various countries.

By the end of the 1980s, the Anarchist Black Cross movement began to grow again. Seven chapters had formed throughout the United Kingdom, with one in Scotland. ABC groups formed in the Nordic countries of Denmark, Finland, and Sweden. In North America, four chapters emerged in Toronto, Vancouver, New York, and San Lorenzo, California. The San Lorenzo group prided itself on being the first Anarchist Black Cross in the United States but was prevented from having the honor of being the first North American ABC chapter due to one forming in Toronto just before them in 1982. The San Lorenzo ABC was clearly unaware of the now-defunct chapters in

AMEDEO BERTOLO

Chicago and Seattle. Other groups also formed in Athens, Greece, as well as in Brisbane, Australia.[50]

By December 1987, the first Anarchist Black Cross conference was organized in Leeds, England. All ABC groups in England were represented, which included Oxford, Plymouth, Liverpool, Bolton, Leeds, Sheffield, and London. Out of the discussion in the conference, it was decided that the groups would not form as a proper anarchist federation but would act as an informal network of anarchist militants.[51]

New ABC publications begin to emerge. Out of the conference in England, it was decided the *Internal Bulletin of the Anarchist Black Cross* would be published to increase dialogue among ABC groups and coordinate global campaigns for anarchist prisoners, such as Katsuhisa Omori, the Vancouver Five, and Noel and Marie Murray. The Denmark group published a magazine, *Rekyl* (Recoil). The Melbourne group also published a magazine called *Black and Blue*.

In 1989, the International Black Cross, an ABC organization that helped to coordinate groups internationally, established the Emergency Response Network (ERN) to mobilize a global call to action in support of anarchist prisoners. Within a few months of being established, the ERN was used in response to the torture of two Greek anarchists, Yannis Petropoulos and Paraskevas Arapostathis. ABC groups and allies throughout the world demonstrated outside of Greek embassies and centers of commerce, forcing the Greek government to address the mistreatment of the anarchists.[52] The ERN was used in North America the following year after anarchist John Perotti called for a hunger strike in response to the increased repression, beatings, and murders of prisoners in US prisons.[53]

GIUSEPPE PINELLI

In August 1994, the first North American Anarchist Black Cross conference was held in New York. Roughly ten groups had formed in recent years throughout the continent, and the conference was called to discuss ways of improving coordination. One of the major topics was the reestablishing of the ERN, which was no longer functioning as it was designed. A proposal was also put forward to establish a long-term project, the Control Unit Monitoring Project (CUMP), to expose the harsh and brutal characteristics of control units, such as isolation; sensory deprivation; limited access to visitations, mail, and phone calls; and increased security measures against those prisoners held in the control units. The project aimed to identify existing control units and work to stop the development of any new control units.

After the conference, three ABC groups (New Jersey in Paterson, New Jersey; Nightcrawler in the Bronx; and Fourth World in Newark, New Jersey) began to form a regional ABC network. The network established the "Warchest," a fund that was designed to consistently provide funds to those political prisoners who receive little or no financial aid.[54] The conference also started a conversation about establishing a stronger organizational relationships among ABC groups. In May 1995, four ABC groups (New Jersey; the Bronx; Washington, DC; and Brew City in Milwaukee) came together to form the Anarchist Black Cross Federation (ABCF). The ABCF embraced the Warchest established by the New Jersey group, continued to maintain the project for the next thirty years, and is still thriving today.

Ideological and personal disputes shaped the North American ABC movement over the next several decades, with various other anarchist prisoner support networks and ABC formations being established. Around the time of the ABCF formation, Raze the Walls, another organization that provided prisoner aid, began to establish a network. The organization functioned until about the turn of the century before fading away. Tensions between specific individuals and chapters of Raze the Walls and the ABCF undermined any effective cooperation between the two organizations throughout their coexistence. Still, some chapters of the Raze the Walls Network worked so well with some of the ABCF chapters that they eventually joined the ABCF.

In July 2002, a conference was held in Austin, Texas, to form the Anarchist Black Cross Network (ABCN). Over the next several years, long-standing personal and ideological disputes among individuals and groups fostered a deep hostility between the ABCF and the ABCN. Some of the ideological disputes were over the ABCF's general support of all "class war" political prisoners and not just anarchist political prisoners. The ABCN took a position that the ABC movement should support anarchist prisoners and should not provide support for those who are not considered anarchists. A few within the ABCN also took the position that all prisoners should be considered political prisoners, a view that was strongly opposed by members of the ABCF, who felt that the term "political prisoner" should be applied only to those who were arrested or targeted because of their political activity or beliefs and who often faced considerably harsher treatment and sentences because of this fact.

However, one the greatest tensions between the ABCF and the ABCN was over the ABCF's refusal to recognize two anarchist prisoners, Harold H. Thompson and Chris Plummer, as political prisoners. The ABCF felt that both individuals made claims related to their political activity that were questionable or were proven to be false. Furthermore, it was discovered that one of Harold H. Thompson's alleged actions was in fact a domestic violence case. While the ABCF was not critical of the anarchist community supporting either individual as anarchist prisoners, it was vocal about the support for them as political prisoners. Thompson, Plummer, and their supporters were equally vocal about their criticism of ABCF's position, arguing that the ABCF provides more support to other movements than to its own. When Plummer was released from prison, he helped to establish the ABCN, which helped to foster the tension between the two groups.

The disagreement over supporting political prisoners outside of the anarchist movement is nothing new in the ABC movement and has existed as far back as 1924 when Alexander Berkman was corresponding with Lillie Sarnoff of the Anarchist Red Cross in New York. Sarnoff was critical of Berkman for using his standing within the anarchist and revolutionary movements to raise money for anarchists and Left Socialist-Revolutionaries imprisoned in Russia when, in her view, they should have only been raising money for anarchists. Berkman, who was working with the Joint Committee for the Defense of the Revolutionaries Imprisoned in Russia, argued that support for individuals based solely on their identification of being an anarchist would be foolish since some who identified themselves as anarchists could not be considered as such in Berkman and Sarnoff's sense of the word. He argued that some self-identified anarchists (individualists, Stirnerians, universalists, Gordinists) are "cranks who do more harm than good."[55] He further argued that many of the Left Socialist-Revolutionaries were good revolutionaries who deserved support.

While Berkman and Sarnoff still seemed to have the ability to work together, the hostility that developed between the ABCF and the ABCN fostered disdain and distrust between the two organizations for several years. In August 2003, in response to an open letter of solidarity issued by the Los Angeles chapter of the ABCF, the Break the Chains in Eugene, Oregon (a group associated with the ABCN), invited members of the Los Angeles group to an ABCN conference. At the conference, individuals from the ABCF and the ABCN sat down to discuss how to move past the conflict and began to develop a working relationship. The tension between the two organizations continued to dissipate as the years progressed. ABCN continued to function for several years, but like Raze the Walls they eventually faded away. The ABCF has remained an active organization and has continued to build working relationships with those ABC chapters that are not affiliated with the federation.

Other regional ABC federations and networks were also forming around the world during this time. Roughly at the time the ABCF was formed, ABC groups began to form in Spain. However, a series of incidents forced the groups on the Iberian Peninsula to pause their plans to form some type of network or federation. But in December 2003, the Spanish federation of ABC groups was formed. The new federation reached out to other ABC organizations, including those in Latin America. With the exception of the ABC Latino-Americano in Miami during the early 1990s, the ABC movement had little or no presence in Latin American countries until around the turn of the twenty-first century. Chapters soon emerged in Argentina, Costa Rica, Columbia, Uruguay, Venezuela, and Mexico. The Spanish federation of ABC groups collaborated with ABC groups in Venezuela and in other countries to form La Red Latina de CNAs (the Latin Network of ABCs), a network of Spanish-speaking ABC organizations that worked together to provide aid to one another and to anarchist prisoners in those regions.[56]

In June 2001, ABC groups from around Europe met in Ghent, Belgium, to discuss the formation of a network of ABC organizations. Groups from Italy, Poland, the Czech Republic, France, Luxembourg, the United Kingdom, Holland, Germany, and Belgium agreed that a network of autonomous groups would be formed to further the aims of the ABC.[57]

But much like the previous waves of the ABC movement, it would not take long for the emerging movement to find itself in conflict with the state in virtually every place the organization appeared.

In the United States, both the ABCF and the ABCN experienced harassment by local and federal agencies. Even prior to the formation of the ABCF, the New Jersey ABC found itself the target of political violence. The ABC group formed out of the Paterson Anarchist Collective, an organization that, among other things, ran the Right to Existence bookstore. The two organizations shared the same membership with the ABC working out of the bookstore. In October 1992, after a series of incidents only days apart, including a raid by more than a dozen police officers, the bookstore's door was hit by eight bullets.[58] Less than a year later, in August of 1993, the window of the bookstore was smashed the day after a confrontation with police.[59]

In January 1996, the Jacksonville chapter of the ABCF was raided on two separate occasions. Police seized computers, weapons, and other material with the intent of discovering the activities of the organization. Members of the group were arrested and charged with felony criminal

GEORG VON RAUCH

mischief in connection with political graffiti, which carried a possible five-year sentence. The charges were eventually dropped.[60]

Members of the New Jersey and Jacksonville, Florida, ABCF chapters were also suspected of hiding Azikikwe Onipedo (known to authorities as Arthur Washington Jr.), a member of the Black Liberation Army, a Black revolutionary guerilla organization that was active in the United States in the 1970s and 1980s. Onipedo was wanted in connection with a 1989 shootout with a New Jersey state trooper.[61] He was placed on the FBI's Ten Most Wanted list the same year. Agents harassed family members, neighbors, and landlords of ABCF members despite having no concrete evidence.

In February 2005, the director of the FBI, Robert Mueller, identified the ABCF, during a Senate Committee on Intelligence, as a potential threat to national security that would continue to be an issue for law enforcement. Mueller went on to say "the ABCF has continued to organize, recruit, and train anarchists in the tactical use of firearms."[62]

Members of the organization were unaware that the FBI and the federal government had convened a federal grand jury hearing to determine whether federal charges could be filed against members of the Los Angeles and Jacksonville chapters for possession of illegal firearms and "engaging in violent crimes through either the promotion of, or participation in, weapons training to advance armed revolution similar to that of the Black Liberation Army (BLA)."[63] What Mueller and the FBI were referencing was the Tactical Defense Caucus of the Anarchist Black Cross Federation, a section of the organization that trained in self-defense. The caucus was formed after a series of

TOMMY WEISSBECKER

attacks by far-right groups against anarchists, including the assassination of two antiracist skinheads in Las Vegas. All self-defense training was completely legal, but that did not stop the federal government's attempt to criminalize the intentions of the caucus or the larger ABCF.

In September 2005, Neil Batelli of the Jacksonville ABCF was detained by the FBI after the US government's assassination of Los Macheteros leader, Filiberto Ojeda Rios. FBI agents demanded that the ABCF member use his contacts in the Puerto Rican independence movement to determine the response of the Los Macheteros and attempted to get him to reveal additional information about other organizations and ABCF members. It was later discovered that Batelli was befriended by an informant who tried to persuade the ABCF member to illegally sell him a gun. This highlighted the lengths the government would go to in order to entrap members of the organization.

In August 2007, New Jersey ABC member, Mathias Bolton, was attacked by two Jersey City police officers after the police were called to Bolton's apartment building due to a suspected break-in. Bolton, unaware that the plainclothesmen were police, resisted as they tried to force Bolton back into the building. Bolton was thrown down a flight of stairs and the police proceeded to kick, punch, and drag him along the pavement. He was then arrested and charged with assault and resisting arrest. Bolton filed a civil suit against the officers.

Prosecutors and the defense attorneys for the police officers in the civil case attempted to use Bolton's connections with ABCF and Black revolutionary groups, like the Black Liberation Army, to suggest that Bolton attacked the police officers as some type of revolutionary act. Despite the baselessness of the claim, their case was bolstered when the FBI provided them with Bolton's entire FBI file. The prosecution against Bolton and the defense attorneys in the civil case were now able to support their argument with years of FBI monitoring of Bolton's activities and connections with various groups and individuals within different revolutionary movements.

As Bolton's cases were moving through the courts, they were soon hit with another twist. In 2008, some of the officers involved in Bolton's assault were swept up in a New York Police Department steroid ring. At least 248 officers and firefighters were supplied steroids, growth hormones, and other testosterone-boosting drugs from a Jersey City doctor before he died around the same time as Bolton's assault. Two of the officers involved in Mathias's case were accused in the investigation.[64] Now the media and Bolton's defense began to paint the incident as a police assault fueled by a steroid-induced rage. With the FBI assisting the police officers in Mathias's case and the officers' reputation now in question, both sides withdrew their case against the other.

In February 2010, the national media would try to connect the ABCF with al-Qaeda, when Ojore Lutalo, a former political prisoner and member of the New Jersey ABCF, was detained on a train in Colorado. The government claimed that he made several terrorist threats while talking on his cell phone to a member of the Lancaster, Pennsylvania, ABCF. It was allegedly during this conversation that he referred to al-Qaeda. Despite the accusation, no charges were ever filed. However, the national media took advantage of the incident, associating Lutalo and the ABCF with global terrorism.[65]

Chapters of the ABCN also found themselves under surveillance. In 2004, the Joint Terrorist Task Force was monitoring various antiwar organizations in the Denver area who were protesting the Iraq war. Denver ABCN was one of many groups being monitored because of their activities. The degree of surveillance was not revealed until the Denver ACLU requested information through the Freedom of Information Act. The same year, the Chicago Police Department publicly admitted to having infiltrated several progressive and left-wing organizations, including the ABCN's Chicago chapter.

Shortly after FBI director Robert Mueller referenced the ABCF in the 2005 hearing, Michele McPhee from the *Boston Herald* contacted the Los Angeles ABCF to get a response regarding Mueller's claim that the ABCF sympathizes with al-Qaeda. This was not the claim made by Mueller; rather, he stated that "U.S.-based black separatist groups follow radical variants of Islam, and in some cases express solidarity with al-Qaeda and other international terrorist groups."[66] As an anarchist organization, the ABCF did not adhere to any Black separatist ideology and was not sympathetic to al-Qaeda. However, McPhee seemed determined to connect the two organizations despite being shown her error by the representative of the ABCF.

After ABCF representatives refused to go on record due to McPhee's clear misrepresentation of the facts, she contacted the ABCN group in Boston. Both the Boston and Los Angeles groups had made it clear that the Boston chapter of the ABCN had no affiliation with the ABCF. This did not stop McPhee from trying to get a quote from members of the Boston group for her story about the ABCF. Her article stated the ABCF was an emerging revolutionary group hell-bent on creating a classless society, using armed resistance if necessary, and that the ABCF had members in Boston who had distributed a flier suggesting locations to attack, including the Boston Police Headquarters, the

FBI office, the IRS building, a military recruitment center, and several corporate sites. McPhee then drew the connection to al-Qaeda by taking Mueller's quote out of context, suggesting that the quote was in reference to ABCF. While the article ended with a quote from a member of the Boston group stating that the organization did not sympathize with al-Qaeda, the damage was done to both the ABCF and the ABCN. The Boston group would continue to be monitored by local police and the FBI for several years after the article.[67]

In Europe, the relationship between the ABC movement and the underground movement would again lead to the arrests and imprisonment of members. On June 28, 2004, a shootout took place near a German border crossing between police and two Spanish anarchists, José Fernández Delgado and Gabriel Pombo da Silva. Both men had escaped from Spanish prisons. The two men were driving with Begoña Pombo da Silva (Gabriel's sister) and Bart De Geeter, a member of the Ghent Anarchist Black Cross. Begoña Pombo da Silva was quickly detained, but the three men escaped before eventually being arrested. They would later be known as the Aachen Four. The three men were charged with nine counts of attempted murder, two counts of hostage taking, armed robbery, planning of a robbery, and serious traffic violations. Begoña Pombo da Silva was charged with "violent resistance." Fernández Delgado was sentenced to fourteen years. Gabriel Pombo da Silva was given thirteen years. Bart De Geeter received only three and a half years. Begoña Pombo da Silva was sentenced to ten months in prison.[68]

The Italian government spent over a decade trying to connect the Anarchist Black Cross with the underground anarchist movement. In November 2002, DIGOS agents

(Italian political police) conducted a series of raids in connection to a member of the Italian Anarchist Black Cross. During one of the raids, agents seized a hard drive, numerous pamphlets, brochures, newspapers, and nearly three hundred copies of *Croce Nera Anarchica*, a magazine published by the Italian ABC group. A year and a half later, on May 26, 2005, police arrested several members of the ABC group (Massimo Leonardi, Danilo Cremonese, Valentina Speziale, Claudia Cospito, and Stefano Del Moro). They were accused of engaging in, or planning, a series of bombings, including the one at the Court of Viterbo on January 19, 2004. They were also accused of an attempted explosion on October 23, 2003, targeting the Center for Social Services for Adults and the ransacking of a McDonald's on February 13, 1999, following a demonstration in Viterbo. The government also shut down the ABC website. As part of the arrests, which the government called "Operation Croce Nera," the DIGOS also engaged in a series of raids targeting anarchists throughout Italy in which four others (Marco Feruzzi, Simone Del Moro, Sergio Maria Stéfani, and David Santini) were arrested and charged. All were eventually acquitted except for Feruzzi, Leonardi, and Simone Del Moro who were sentenced to nine, six, and three years respectively.[69]

On September 6, 2016, the DIGOS engaged in another series of raids, over thirty in total, of anarchist homes. These raids, known as "Operation Scripta Manent" were in response to a series of actions claimed by the guerilla group, Informal Anarchist Federation. The group engaged in an armed struggle campaign throughout the previous decade, targeting government structures and agents.

The Italian government initially arrested five anarchists, three of whom were Anarchist Black Cross members who had previously been arrested in Operation Croce Nera (Alessandro Mercogliano, Danilo Cremonese, and Valentina Speziale). Also arrested was Marco Bisesti, an editor of *Croce Nera Anarchica*, and Anna Beniamino. Two other imprisoned anarchists were also informed of charges, Alfred Cospito, brother of Claudia Cospito, and Nicola Gai. Shortly afterwards, Daniele Cortelli, another ABC member who had been part of the "Operation Croce Nera" trial was arrested and accused of possessing material to manufacture explosive devices. The DIGOS discovered batteries and a handbook for electricians during a raid of his home.[70]

In June 2017, seven additional Italian anarchists were arrested, including Stefano Del Moro and Claudia Cospito from the Operation Croce Nera case. Three others, Alessandro Audisio, Pasquale "Lello" Valittuti, and Omar Nioi, were also members of the Anarchist Black Cross and were editors of the *Croce Nera Anarchica*. They were charged with subversive association, criminal solicitation, and the publication of anarchist material. The others who were arrested were associated with the websites radioAzione and anarhija.info, and, like those who produced *Croce Nera Anarchica*, they were accused of publishing articles in sympathy with the Informal Anarchist Federation and for supporting those incarcerated who were allegedly associated with the guerilla organization. In total, twenty-three anarchists were charged for alleged association or advocacy and support of alleged members of the Informal Anarchist Federation.

In April 2019, eighteen of those charged were acquitted. Alfred Cospito received an additional twenty years added to his prison sentence. Anna Beniamino was sentenced to seventeen years. Her sentenced was reduced by six months on appeal. Nicola Gai received nine years in prison. His sentence was reduced to one year and one month on appeal. Alessandro Mercogliano, one of the ABC members arrested in the "Operation Croce Nera" case, received a five-year sentence. He was later acquitted on appeal. Marco Bisesti was sentenced to five years, but his sentenced was reduced to one year and nine months after an appeal for "incitement to commit crimes" in relation to the Anarchist Black Cross.[71]

As mentioned earlier, the chapters on the Iberian Peninsula had a series of setbacks that prevented them from moving forward with their intention to better cooperate with other ABC groups. When ABC groups first began to form throughout the region around 1996, there were several groups scattered around the region and a very strong chapter in Madrid.

The organization remained largely under the authorities' radar until the start of the twenty-first century. In the early months of 2000, several mail bombs were sent to various right-wing journalists and the president of the Movement Against Intolerance, a state-backed organization against terrorism. Within the packages were leaflets calling for the end of FIES units. FIES stands for Ficheros de Internos de Especial Seguimiento (Files of Inmates Under Special Monitoring). The units were established to hold prisoners who have been imprisoned for insurrectionary acts against the state, those who have been labeled as "terrorists," or were members of armed groups. The units later included violent prisoners and drug dealers. Like control units in the United States, FIES units have been criticized for their inhumane conditions. FIES unit restrictions include twenty-two hours of solitary confinement a day. All details of each individual's existence and communication are monitored and recorded.

The police suggested to the media that an anarchist "cell" working closely with prisoners in FIES units, was responsible for the packages. Police implied that the cell had been corresponding with an anarchist in the FIES units, Claudio Lavazza, through two other prisoners, Ghibert Ghislain and Santiago Cobos. Allegedly, the two prisoners would communicate the targets to Eduardo García and Estefanía Maurette Díaz, the partner of Santiago Cobos, who would then mail the bombs to the unsuspecting targets.[72]

Police arrested the two on November 8, 2000. Both were charged with sending seven letter bombs to six journalists. García had been involved in the ABC and other antiprison organizations in Madrid.[73] Despite allegations in the media that Ghibert Ghislain and Santiago Cobos were involved in the anarchist movement, reports from the anarchist movement were that it had no connection with the two and that Maurette Diaz's only crime was being partners with Cobos.

In January 2004, García was sentenced to four years in prison for possession of gunpowder. He was found not guilty of the bombings due to lack of evidence. All other parties, including Estefania Maurette Diaz, had their charges dropped.[74]

During the time that García was awaiting trial, another incident occurred that would put the Anarchist Black Cross in the headlines in Spain. Between July and November 2002, a series of arrests took place throughout Spain and France, targeting members of the Communist Party of Spain (Reconstituted) and GRAPO (First of October Antifascist Resistance Groups). The Communist Party of Spain (Reconstituted) was a clandestine Marxist-Leninist organization that broke away from the Communist Party of Spain. GRAPO acted as the armed wing of the organization.

On July 18, 2002, the Spanish Civil Guard arrested two alleged GRAPO members, Fernando Pérez López and Jesús Merino del Viejo, in Madrid. The National Court ordered the imprisonment of Jesús Merino del Viejo, among others for their participation in GRAPO, but Fernando Pérez López had been released. It was later discovered that Fernando Pérez López had been a Civil Guard who had been infiltrating leftist groups since November 1997.[75]

Fernando Pérez López arrived in Madrid in November 1997, from Barcelona. He quickly began to build relationships with individuals in the Association of Relatives and Friends of Political Prisoners (AFAPP). In March 1999, he joined the Anarchist Black Cross in Madrid.[76]

According to accounts of members of the ABC, his involvement with the organization did not last long since it seemed that he had more interest in supporting GRAPO prisoners than in the anarchist and social prisoners. He soon went back to the AFAPP and members of the ABC soon lost contact with him. It was not until his reported arrest and release was his true identity became clear. In January 2003, the man formerly known as Fernando Pérez López did an interview for the Spanish newspaper *La Razón* in which he confirmed that he had been a Civil Guard who successfully infiltrated various left-wing organizations, including the Anarchist Black Cross and GRAPO. It was also later revealed that Fernando Pérez López was directly connected in the arrest of Eduardo García.[77]

On March 13, 2003, based on the fabricated charges against Eduardo García, the information provided by the informant known as Fernando Pérez López, and the media spin connecting the Anarchist Black Cross to GRAPO, a judge declared the ABC in Spain to be an illegal organization. He argued that the ABC is part of the recruitment machinery of the GRAPO. The organization issued a statement that read in part, "We have never been part of the structure of any party, nor are we the recruiting apparatus for anyone. Since we are not Marxists, we are anarchists and our ideas lead us to position ourselves against any hierarchy or authority, as well as any vanguard or army. If we are clear about one thing, it is that as an autonomous and anarchist organization we do not submit to the general secretary of any political party, no matter how Marxist it may be."[78]

Despite the government declaring the Anarchist Black Cross an illegal organization, the Federation of Anarchist Black Cross on the Iberian Peninsula persisted. The media continued to connect the ABC with bombings throughout Spain. In 2013, Greek anarchists claimed a bombing at La Almudena Cathedral in Madrid. A *La Razón* article alleged a connection between the ABC in Madrid and an international anarchist movement responsible for the attacks. In 2016, several activists were arrested during an action at the carnivals in Madrid. The media associated one of those arrested, Raúl García, with the ABC and tried to connect them with the ETA, a Basque separatist guerilla group.

While the ABC movement was slow to develop in the Latin American region, it was not able to remain undetected by government agencies who were quick to tie the organization to various incidents as a way of attacking the anarchist movement as a whole. For example, in Bogotá, Colombia, a young anarchist named Nicolás Neira Álvarez was killed during a May Day 2005 protest after being beaten by the Mobile Anti-Riot Squad (ESMAD). The Bogotá police attempted to seize the moment by shifting the blame onto the anarchist movement, indirectly accusing the ABC in Bogotá of being responsible for the death. The anarchist movement began receiving a constant barrage of threats and harassment. Several anarchists were detained a few weeks after Nicolás Neira Álvarez was killed and death threats were sent to lawyers closely related the ABC chapter.[79]

In Uruguay, on July 27, 2005, after a Molotov cocktail and tar bombs were used against the Italian Consulate, the Italian Institute of Culture, and the Italian Chamber of Commerce in Uruguay, various conservative media outlets accused the Uruguayan ABC of being responsible for the attacks in solidarity with the anarchist movement in Italy.

On December 1, 2012, Mexico witnessed a series of clashes between police and protesters over the election of Enrique Peña Nieto. In Mexico City, the federal police were brutal in their attack against protesters, arresting nearly a hundred people, with dozens injured. The attorney general of Mexico City and the mayor attributed the violence to three groups: the Anarchist Black Bloc, Anarchist Black Cross, and the Anarchist Student Coordinator Collective. In response to the accusations of violence, the Anarchist Black Cross and the Anarchist Student Coordinator Collective held a press conference stating that none of their members were arrested during the demonstration but that they stood in solidarity with those arrested.

In November 2014, another demonstration in Mexico City resulted in a Metrobús bus and station, as well as the doors of the National Palace, being set on fire. Eighteen people in total were detained and the local police and media identified five organizations as being responsible. Once again, the Anarchist Black Cross was accused of being responsible for the attacks.[80]

Five months later, on March 27, 2015, the National Electoral Institute (INA) was bombed in Puebla, Mexico. An anonymous group announced that the action was the beginning of the so-called Black June campaign to boycott the upcoming elections in June.[81] After the attack, with additional actions that followed, CISNE (the Center for Research and National Security) issued a public warning that anarchist groups intended to destabilize and sabotage the upcoming local and national elections. In the warning several radical and anarchist groups were mentioned, including ABC–Mexico City. In response, the group had to issue another statement condemning the ongoing harassment by the federal government targeting anarchists and the Anarchist Black Cross.[82]

In 2003, the Black Cross, which was once declared illegal in Russia, returned to the country when a chapter was formed in Moscow. It was soon followed with the St. Petersburg group being organized in August 2007.[83] The St. Petersburg group published a newspaper called the *Black Cross.* In March 2012, Antti Rautiainen, a Finnish-born member of the Moscow Anarchist Black Cross was ordered to leave Russia by the Federal Migration Service of Russia for "making statements for the overthrow of the constitutional order" and for being a member of the group Autonomous Action.[84] In February 2024, the Ministry of Justice declared the Anarchist Black Cross Federation to be an undesirable organization.[85] Initial reports seemed to suggest that the banned organization is the Anarchist Black Cross Federation based in the United States. Although affected by this declaration, the Moscow and St. Petersburg chapters currently exist and continue the tradition of anarchist prison support in the birthplace of the movement.

CONCLUSION

As this book is being currently republished, the Anarchist Black Cross movement is as vibrant as ever. The spirit of mutual aid and solidarity has continued to guide the movement forward and there is hope that this will endure for many decades to come. Projects like ABCF's Warchest have continued for over thirty years, providing aid directly to political prisoners in North America. Other projects like the International Anti-Fascist Defense Fund and the International Anarchist Defense Fund have formed providing similar support. Since 1999, ABC groups and allies have organized Running Down the Walls, a 5k run to raise awareness and support for political prisoners. These runs take place in cities and prisons throughout North America, celebrating solidarity across the prison walls. It is our hope that the event will spread to other continents in the coming years. Since 2010, the international anarchist movement has come together every June 11 to support long-term anarchist prisoners. It has become a global act of rebellion and solidarity.

When Yelensky set off to write this book, his original title was *Shadows in the Struggle for Equality*. However, during the publishing of the book, the title was changed to *In the Struggle for Equality*. A decision has been made for the republishing of this edition to return it to the original title.

When originally released, this book was the most comprehensive account of the history of the Anarchist Black Cross. The fact that such a contribution would be given by Boris Yelensky would be the only natural conclusion. No person, beyond his wife, Bessie Yelensky, had dedicated as much of their life to the organization and to the anarchist prisoners it supported.

But since the publication of the first edition, the Anarchist Black Cross has continued to flourish. Others, such as Albert Meltzer and Stuart Christie have helped to breathe new life into the organization. Some, such as Giuseppe Pinelli, Georg von Rauch, and Thomas Weissbecker, have died while being active in the Anarchist Black Cross. And many more have faced the repressive weight of the state because of their dedication to aid those incarcerated behind prison walls.

When Yelensky died, it had been seven years since the Anarchist Black Cross was reformed. If there is a question as to whether Yelensky was aware of the organization's rebirth, the answer can be found in the second issue of the *Bulletin of the Anarchist Black Cross*, in November 1968, where it is reported that Yelensky wrote to the new organization to congratulate them on its revival. Yelensky did travel to London in August 1969, so it is hard to imagine he did not contact the members of the new organization, but it is unknown if this happened.

As was the case with the first edition of *In the Struggle for Equality*, this edition will be the most complete document regarding the history of the Anarchist Black Cross. Additional information has been added in the endnotes and additional appendixes to enhance the work that Yelensky put forward. It can be argued that it is done so that Yelensky can finally be given credit for the contributions he made for his dedication to the principle of mutual aid. All the new material, footnotes, appendixes, and illustrations are wrapped around and added to the work that Yelensky put down. As we have continued to do, we have built upon the work of those before us. Through their inspiration, we strive for a better world.

INTRODUCTION

This book has been produced because the Publication Committee believes that the story of the Anarchist Red Cross, and of other rescue and aid organizations, should be told. The time will soon come when those who lived through these experiences will no longer be here to tell their story. Therefore writers, editors, and teachers have combined to help Boris Yelensky produce the book, and many others have given generously to care for the costs. It is hoped that the future generations may find this work interesting and may profit from the experiences related here.

This little book gives a picture of life among the Jewish immigrants from Eastern Europe who were arriving in America in the early years of this century in large numbers. To some extent they transplanted the culture they had known in Europe. But in this country the old pressures were off, and new pressures took their place, causing misunderstanding, and difficulties in adjustment.

Of the many interesting stories, which have been, and will be, told of these people, one of the most valuable is this account of a sympathetic movement to aid the persecuted comrades "back home." How was this organized? How did the comrades respond? These immigrants came seeking liberty, as had the original Pilgrim Fathers; their problems were no less difficult, and their response was perhaps no less noble. We would like to know more about the life of the early Pilgrims; the time may come when there is great curiosity about the life of the largest numbers of liberty-seeking immigrants who came three centuries later.

These alert, fearless, working people in New York, Philadelphia, Chicago, Los Angeles, Detroit, and other cities, responded to Yelensky's appeal. They had been the vehicle through which the apostles of revolution and social change carried their ideal into the trade union movement, into cooperatives, into the education of the young, and into plans for international federation and world association. Perhaps no society could live up to the utopian visions they had conceived, but they were not ready to settle for anything less than a world of liberty, of brotherhood, and of peace. Thus, even in America they continued to study and work for their ideal and to maintain a sense of ideological solidarity.

We are fortunate in having this story told by one of the most prominent actors in it, Boris Yelensky. He was born in the Caucasus of Jewish ancestry, amid the fires of Russian Revolution. In consequence he was not taught Hebrew, and it was not until he came to America as a young boy [that] he learned Yiddish. In Philadelphia he became an active member of the Radical Library. This library was more than a store of books; it was an association, one of the most important centers of the intellectual radical movement in the early years of this century. The leader of this library at the time was Joseph Cohen, writer, lecturer, editor, and organizer of cooperative communities. Yelensky received his social education from Cohen, and his practical experience in this Radical Library.

Boris Yelensky is approaching the age of seventy as this is written. For almost fifty years he devoted all his energies to the movement of rescue and aid for those who suffered at the hands of tyrants in many parts of the world. He worked prodigiously to raise money for thousands of packages to be sent to Europe. He wrote innumerable letters on behalf of the cause. He devoted a lifetime to help build a better world and to form and sustain an international chain of assistance for the oppressed.

In 1949 a booklet celebrating the sixtieth birthday of Yelensky was published, containing the tributes of many friends. Rudolf Rocker, the internationally famous anarchist, author of *Nationalism and Culture* says there: "Yelensky is ... a brave man who always had an aim in life and the strength to fight for it ... he has never been idle and does his work with love and devotion."

The tribute of M. [Morris] Beresin in that booklet is especially significant. He says:

When I arrived in the United States in 1911, a fugitive from a hard-labor sentence in Siberia, my first thought was to devise some means of extending aid to our comrades who were languishing in Russian prisons. I promptly proceeded to have a noticed inserted in the Russian-language newspapers requesting any coworkers in our ideological movement who were located in Philadelphia ... to come to a meeting. Among those who attended that gathering was Yelensky. Our first step was the ... organization of the "Anarchist Red Cross" ... Yelensky is one of the most ardent and dynamic workers in our Movement; he has not for a single moment deviated from his ideological course; He has not allowed himself to become assimilated ... by the American Bourgeois spirit. This intransigence of his ... was responsible for the fact that in time he became to be recognized as more than a person. He became a veritable "institution."

Beresin points out that Yelensky is a product of the Russian revolutionary movement and anarchist thought, and says, "the Russian Revolutionary Movement embraced representatives of all social classes, from the highest nobility down to the humblest proletarian and peasant. In the revolutionary ranks were found outstanding thinkers, scholars, writers, orators, and a host of plain, common people. But all of them, regardless of their social or intellectual status, were permeated by the same spirit of revolutionary idealism and freedom, by the same impulse to risk and sacrifice, if need be, their lives for the cause they held dear. Boris Yelensky is one of the very few surviving 'pure specimens,' of that heroic era."

Since America was not in a revolutionary period, the anarchist movement here appeared quixotic rather than heroic. Yet the Russian heroes were a very legend to the anarchists who crowded halls to hear lectures on the writings of Kropotkin, Bakunin, Tolstoy, Proudhon, and Johann Most. In America generally these anarchists were vigorously denounced for their beliefs and actions. The teaching of anarchy was considered a sin, and it became really dangerous to even peek into anarchist literature. For most people "anarchy" was made a synonym for "chaos." It therefore becomes necessary to give some idea of what anarchy means.

Anarchists believe in such freedom of thought that they have never been willing to adopt a binding statement of beliefs. Nevertheless, anarchists feel that their ideal of freedom has been an increasing influence upon the political thinking, the education, the social planning of all nations since the turn of the century. They feel that they have been persecuted because they were the gadflies of progress, rather than because they were wrong.

The *Encyclopedia Britannica* has a quite full and sympathetic account of anarchy. We would particularly call the reader's attention to the *Encyclopedia of Social Sciences*, which can be found in many libraries, and which has an excellent article on anarchy by Oscar Jászi, a Hungarian scholar who was a teacher at Oberlin College. He gives a comprehensive survey of the history and literature of anarchy, and outlines some ideals which were the center of discussion at the Congress of American Anarchists held in Pittsburgh in 1883, as follows:

> (1) To establish justice, that is, equality and reciprocity, in all human relations by the complete elimination of the state, or by the greatest possible minimization of its activities, and its replacement by an entirely free and spontaneous cooperation between individuals, groups, regions and nations. (2) Our unbearable social and moral evils cannot be cured, or even alleviated by the state, which is necessarily an instrument of domination and exploitation. (3) All reforms from above are worthless and can only augment our present misfortune. Only the principle of federalism, beginning with the humblest of human relations and ascending to the highest international cooperation, can establish a new society. (4) This new society can only be the result of a revolutionary action in the soul, or on the sociopolitical life, which will destroy the state ... and all coercive systems whatsoever.

In the light of experience with the Bolshevik Revolution, the anarchist today no longer plans political revolution, but emphasizes the "revolution of the soul," which treasures freedom, and personal responsibility for moral and political action. Such a revolution is needed today more than ever.

However, the groups of which Yelensky speaks, in the early years, were anticipating a world revolutionary social change. Wherever they could find a platform or could make a demonstration they were eager and ready to present their ideas. Yet, outside of agitation, they lived rather ordinary lives and fulfilled all obligations as citizens. They believed in libertarian communism—several types of communism were expounded, but the kind that appealed most to this group was Peter Kropotkin's. In Kropotkin's view the state was to be eliminated and the village was to become a real commune, a brotherhood, a family society, the nucleus of a worldwide, humanity-wide organism.

The experience of the Russian Revolution proved to them who was right in the Marx-Bakunin dispute. As they encountered the oppression of Marxist communism in Russia, they came to repudiate violence, and turned increasingly toward a more "spiritual revolution." The underground tactics, which had been necessary in Russia, were gradually eliminated from their thinking. They became interested in the defense of civil liberties in America, in opposing the standardization of art and education through the controls of the ruling-class group, and in supporting efforts for broader international unity.

In Russia they had been part of a revolutionary move-ment, and it was only gradually that they discovered that there was no revolutionary situation here in which they could participate. But wherever liberties were in jeopardy they continued to express their concern, and in particular, they did what they could for those who were being perse-cuted for the cause of freedom in Europe. They attempted to form some communities for the exploration of anarchis-tic principles in practice, but these colonies were not very successful. They did, however, inculcate a love of freedom in their young, and in many people, who were reached by their activities.

Yelensky's story is colored by the fact that there has been division among the forces of freedom everywhere. The project for the relief of anarchists arose because the anarchists were discriminated against by the socialists and communists who had been their comrades in the fight against the Tsar, and later against Franco. The Marxists had larger and stronger organizations, and therefore were able to control popular programs of relief. Under these circumstances, the anarchists were refused aid on the pretense that they were just "bandits." This accusation is a manifestation of the fact that the followers of Marx treated the anarchists in the same way that Marx himself treated Bakunin. Those who know the lives and teachings of the apostles of anarchy—Kropotkin, Bakunin, Malatesta, Tolstoy, Reclus, Michel, and others, know that they repre-sent the most ideal humanism of mankind. Therefore, it is obvious that the accusation of "banditry" is a gratui-tous slander. These accusations, coming from their former comrades, were particularly resented.

The judgments, which Yelensky pronounces on vari-ous individuals and groups, may not always be accepted as accurate. The Publishing Committee feels, however, that Yelensky has earned the right to express his view in his own way. If he is wrong the field is open for others to reply and set the record straight. Right or wrong his feelings explain why he acted as he did in developing the relief organization to which he has devoted his life. The serious student must take these views into account even though this report might need to be balanced with a study of other writings.

Again, today we hear thousands of young people in Hungary, in Poland, and in other parts of the world who want to die for ideas rather than for things. Even a generation brought up under Communist totalitarianism need not be molded forever. The work of the past was not in vain, and it may give inspiration for steadfastness to the principle of liberty in the future. The Anarchist Red Cross, and similar organizations, have made their mark in history, and have performed an undying service in the struggle for liberty and equality.

AUTHOR'S PREFACE

When the Russian Revolution released political prisoners from Tsarist confinement, in 1917, it was supposed that there would be no more persecuted comrades needing relief. The Anarchist Red Cross was dissolved and many of the active participants returned to Russia, taking important documents with them. Of the material that remained, much was confiscated by government agents during the notorious Palmer Raids in 1919 or destroyed by people who wanted to avoid trouble with the authorities. Since then, many have died, and details have been forgotten. Thus, it had been difficult to gather material for earlier parts of our story.

In the desperate struggle of radical groups for survival each party has tended to look after the interest of its own people, and has been indifferent, if not hostile to the welfare of others. We have not intended our report to be an exposé of factionalism; but we have to record the facts in order to provide a foundation for realistic plans and programs of the future.

Our story is primarily a report of what so-called "subversive radicals" have contributed to social development in the United States. Scholars are already doing research in this field, and I hope that what I record may help towards the full acknowledgment of the debt which social progress in America owes to this misunderstood group of immigrants.

I had hoped to include a list of all those who took part in Anarchist relief work, but this has proved impossible. These people have the undying gratitude of the many whose lives were saved. The work was not done for the glory, but because we believed in Mutual Aid.

It has been a pleasure to recall the years when we had such great hopes that in our own lifetime, we would see a world in which political persecution would belong to past history. Our dreams are still far from realization, and it seems, alas, that the noble work of providing mutual aid for our comrades all over the world will continue to be necessary for many years to come.

It has also been pleasant to recollect the enthusiastic activity that existed in so many cities during the old days of the Anarchist Red Cross. There was so much willingness during that period to sacrifice a part of one's life in order to help those comrades who needed assistance in prisons and places of exile. If one compares those visionary years of our youth to the "practical" epoch in which we are now living, one realizes that those young dreamers of the past accomplished much more than the "practical" men of the present. Now that our generation is passing away, and the struggle for Freedom, Humanism, and Justice still lies ahead, I hope that those who take over the work will continue the fine traditions of impartiality and of justice to all those who need help.

I wish to extend my most cordial thanks to all my friends, comrades and groups, and especially to the Philadelphia comrades for their large contributions, which enabled me to complete my book.

I would like to acknowledge my gratitude to Martin Gudell, who suggested that I take up this work; to George Woodcock for his editorial work on the first draft of the manuscript; to my old friend and comrade Beresin for his interest and advice; to Dr. B. for his interest and final editorial work; to Olga Maximoff and Irving S. Abrams for their constructive advice and to Richard Ellington for proofreading the work.

THE NINETEENTH CENTURY

The serious consideration of any aspect of Russian revolutionary history must begin in 1825, the year of the first organized insurrectionary movement, the Decembrist conspiracy against the autocratic rule of Nicholas I. It is true that before the movement arose Russia had already seen many popular uprisings, such as that led by Stenka Rasin on the Volga, and that led by Pugachev, about whom the Russian people still sing their folks songs. But these were spontaneous protests rather than movements based on carefully thought-out social philosophies.

Most of the Decembrist conspirators were officers of the Tsarist army, and some of them were intellectuals influenced by social theories from Western Europe which aroused in them the idea that it was time for the government to give some measure of freedom to its subjects. The Decembrists were in fact men who enjoyed considerable social privileges and a great measure of economic security, but they were not satisfied with these advantages when the vast majority of their fellow countrymen lived in serfdom and oppression; impelled by their ideals, they decided to sacrifice their personal happiness—and even in some cases their lives—in the hope of helping the Russian people.

Their uprising, which took place on the 14th of December 1825, is relevant to our subject because it resulted in the first great exodus of political prisoners to Siberia. Tsar Nicholas I took part personally in the trials of the conspirators and behaved with great cruelty towards these idealists. But his ruthlessness could not destroy the new thoughts of liberty, which the Decembrists injected into Russian intellectual life, and when the impetus of revolt reasserted itself some decades later the new generation of revolutionary intellectuals took up where the Decembrist had left off.

In the 1860s there emerged the Narodniki, a group consisting of students and intellectuals who sacrificed their privileged positions and went among the Russian people to spread the gospel of freedom and to make them understand the true nature of the Tsarist regime. If the Decembrists had shown rather remotely the influence of the Western European ideas, the Narodniki were in full and close contact with the world outside Russia's borders partly through political émigrés, like Herzen, Ogarev, and Bakunin, who, from Western European exiles, established and maintained contact with the movement in their homeland.

Faced with the Narodniki movement, which assumed considerable magnitude, the Tsarist government adopted repressive measures of barbaric thoroughness, and from this period dates the practice of the mass imprisonment of radicals in Russia.

In the seventies the pioneer Narodniki were followed by a new movement, known as the Narodnaya Volya, which concerned itself not only with revolutionary propaganda, as the Narodniki had done, but also with the use of terroristic acts as a means of taking revenge on the Tsars and their officials for the suffering of the Russian people. In turn, it was from the Narodnaya Volya that there emerged the Social-Revolutionary Party, which carried on, with modifications, the traditions of its predecessors. At the same time, there were other movements, such as the Earth-and-Freedom group, which was strongly influenced by the libertarian teachings of Mikhail Bakunin. Marxism appeared relatively late, in the 1880s, when G. Plekhanov left the Earth-and-Freedom group and abandoned Bakunin's teachings to become eventually one of the founders of the Russian Social-Democratic Party, which finally split into two rival groups of Bolsheviks and Mensheviks.

Anarchism as an organized movement appeared in Russia at the end of the 1880s, but the ideas it embodied had already been influential in the revolutionary tradition through the work of those two great libertarians, M. Bakunin and Peter Kropotkin.

Many other revolutionary groups and parties, too numerous for us to mention in detail, arose in Russia during the years before the Revolution of 1917, and all of them contributed their representatives to the political prisons and places of exile. In 1885 the American traveler, George Kennan, visited Russia and was allowed to travel to Siberia. In his return he wrote a moving book, which aroused world-wide protest. Had he visited Siberia thirty years later, in the years immediately preceding the downfall of the Tsarist rule, he would have found the population of the places of exile many times greater.

THE 1905 REVOLUTION

Science suggests that children inherit some of the characteristics of their parents, and if we look at the history of socialism during the past century, we can see that this seems to apply to political parties as well. In the First International Karl Marx and Mikhail Bakunin clashed over the principles and tactics of the labor movements. In order to defeat Bakunin and his associates within the First International, who later became known as the Anarchist movement, Marx and his followers used methods of calumny and vilification, particularly against Bakunin himself, who bore the brunt of the attack against the authoritarian conception of socialism. Down to the present day the followers of Karl Marx, no matter to which faction they may have belonged, have continued to use slander as a method of arousing enmity towards their opponents.

It is true that there have been times when the Social Democrats, or certain groups of them (such as the Mensheviks during the period when they were involved in the bitter strife with the Bolsheviks) have sought to make common cause with the Anarchists. Even in the prisons and places in exile of the Tsarist Russia, the Socialists maintained their resentment towards the Anarchists who were their fellow-fighters in the struggle to free Russia from Tsarist reaction. This resentment went so far that in those prisons where the Social Democrats were in the majority the Anarchists were refused any of the aid that was sent by sympathizers.

The situation in the Russian prisons became particularly acute in the early years of the twentieth century. Immediately before the Russian Revolution of 1905 the activities of the opponents of Tsarism were greatly intensified and the Tsarist government was naturally not idle in retaliation. Every section of the revolutionary movement had many of its members in prisons and exile, and the need for aid grew enormously in comparison with the early years of resistance to Tsarism. Moreover, while formerly the prisoners had been mostly upper-class people, whose families were in a position to help them materially, by the beginning of the twentieth century the change in character of the revolutionary movements led to the appearance of a mass of prisoners drawn from poorer classes, with no resources of their own.

The question of helping the prisoners in fact became a national problem; not only did every section of the socialist movement, both authoritarian and libertarian, raise funds in Russia and abroad, but also the Russian liberal-progressives, and even rich men and aristocrats unattached to any party, felt the obligation to aid political prisoners and exiles. After the 1905 Revolution a non-partisan Red Cross was organized for this purpose, under the leadership of Maxim Gorki's ex-wife, Madam Peshkova.[1] At the same time, in the frequent political trials in Tsarist courts, which drew the attention of the whole world, the most famous Russian lawyers would offer their services to the defense without payment.

In the prerevolutionary times, up to 1917, it often seemed as though the radical, liberal, and progressive groups in Russia had a great unity of feeling; they saw in the liberation of Russia from the corrupt Tsarist government a common aim, and consequently they thought that all political prisoners should be helped. The only exception to this unity of feeling was the Social Democrats with their sectarian policy.

After the failure of the 1905 Revolution the government started the prosecution of all those suspected of taking part in the insurrectionary activities, and the jails and places of exile filled rapidly. Yet despite the strength of the Tsarist government, the political prisoners managed by a bitter struggle in the prisons to establish their rights. I believe it was only in Russia that the political prisoners were at this time acknowledged as a special group, separated from the criminal elements and not compelled to wear prison clothing. Only political prisoners condemned to serve time in *katorga* (hard labor) prisons wore prison clothes and chains; elsewhere the politicals had many privileges. They were allowed to make communal living arrangements, to elect representatives and from among their representatives to choose a *starosta* (headman) whose duty it was to convey grievances to the prison administration and to receive outside help that was sent to the prisoners. But this custom was often abused where the *starosta* was a Social Democrat for he channeled the aid received to members of his own group.

The need to help our comrades in Russian prisons who had been denied aid from the common funds led the Anarchists of Europe and America to organize the Anarchist Red Cross. This organization originated in Europe, which is understandable since people there had more direct contact with whatever was going on in Russia. I have been unable to find the exact date when it began to function there, but the following extract from a letter written by Rudolf Rocker, for many years the treasurer of this organization in London, sets the founding of this organization in the early years of the century:

> The Anarchist Red Cross was founded in the hectic period between 1900 and 1905. All revolutionary parties in Russia organized committees abroad for the assistance of the political prisoners in Russia and Siberia, and those committees took money from everybody, *but our own comrades there received almost nothing.*
>
> That was the reason why the ARC was founded. Only when Vera Figner came to London (she was the treasurer for the political prisoners of the Party of the Socialist Revolutionaries) we had a conference in London with a representative of the SRs and agreed that in all prisons and in Siberia, wherever the Anarchists were in the majority, our fund should send money to all Anarchists and Socialist Revolutionaries, and vice versa.[2]
>
> Rudolf Rocker
> June 2nd, 1956

The first Anarchist Red Cross in the United States was organized in New York in 1907 under the following circumstances. As a result of the reaction, which followed the Revolution of 1905, those who had not yet been arrested began to look for a means of escape from persecution, and a great migration started, to England and especially the United States, where the young people from Russia hoped to find political asylum and liberty. Between 1905 and 1910 tens of thousands of these refugees came to North America, and, since economic conditions were hard and they found themselves among people whose language they could learn only with difficulty, it was natural that their thoughts should linger with their own country and their comrades in prison, and also that, instead of being readily assimilated into their new homes, they should come together in all kinds of Russian and Jewish clubs and societies where the concern for their mother country was maintained at a high level of intensity.

Many of those who reached the United States had participated in the Anarchist movement in Russia, and some had escaped from prisons or places of exile. They brought with them the sad news of the situation of Anarchists in these prisons, where they received little help owing to the Social Democrats being in the majority. This helped create a sympathetic atmosphere for the formation of an ARC in New York; in this the actual pioneers were H. Weinstein[3] and J. Katzenelenbogen,[4] who themselves had been in Russian prisons. The following letter written by H. Weinstein gives many details of how and why they set about this work:

> You want me to write something about the Anarchist Red Cross. A résumé of this subject by Weitzman was published in the *Freie Arbeiter Stimme* in the issue of February 10. What I shall add consists of precise details which friend Weitzman was either unaware of or else had forgotten.[5]
>
> In July or August of 1906, I was placed under arrest in the city of Bialostok. When I arrived at the prison in that city. I met there Jacob Krepleich and a friend of his, a Russian teacher; they likewise

informed me that the organization which then existed in Russia, set up by the Social Democrats to extend aid to all revolutionary captives regardless of political affiliation, was refusing to help the Anarchists; and during the brief period that I remained in the Bialostok prison we received letters from the Grodno jail which gave confirmation of the truth of these statements.

About the time I was released from the prison, Kadel's group of five or six members were sentenced to exile in Siberia. Also, at that time Iza Wishniak was sentenced to Siberian exile.[6] It was urgent to provide them all with clothing and with boots. Naturally money was needed for that purpose, and I knew only too well that the organization existing for that purpose would not contribute to help our comrades. Hence B. Yelin and I,[7] with the cooperation of our coworkers who still remained in Bialostok, undertook to prepare the deportees for their journey, and this task we accomplished efficiently, furnishing them with new boots, linen, and suits of clothing. Often, when we were in the USA, Iza Wishniak would recall what a good job we did equipping our comrades.

In May 1907, I came to the United States. Here I became acquainted with Jacob Katzenelenbogen, whom I had not known in Bialostok. The fact is that for a time he was the only comrade whom I met frequently here in New York, and we had lengthy discussions about the dire situation of our arrested comrades in Russia; for we knew that over there they were receiving no aid from the existing relief organization, nor for our own groups—because very few of our comrades had remained there.

We decided to arrange a concert in the hope of raising some funds for the victims; but how could a mere two men execute such an undertaking? It would be necessary to sell tickets and appeal to organizations for support. I knew very few of our comrades then. But an idea occurred to me—I doubt if I could have carried it out two years later, but at the time it appeared to be the only way to procure help from several persons who had no ideological kinship with us whatsoever.

I don't know whether you are aware that I come from a small town called Orle? I am certain that you have no idea where it is located, but that is of no consequence. However, at that particular time it was extremely important for me to obtain assistance from two persons who had emigrated from my town. Inasmuch as in Kadel's group, which we fitted out for their deportation, one member came from Orle, I contacted two men from Orle who were living in New York City and appealed to what you might call their "civic pride." One of our fellow townsmen, we told them, was in Siberia and must have help. They were acquainted with him, and so my plea was not in vain—they pledged their assistance.

After several conferences and consolations [*sic*], they agreed to our project for a concert to be held in the month of January or else in February 1908—we staged our first concert in the hall on Grand Street.[8] Katzenelenbogen and I went around selling tickets to various organizations; of course, we had to offer some explanations as to why we were seeking aid precisely for Anarchist prisoners. All kinds of questions along this line were put to us and we had to give convincing answers. Fortunately, the two fellow townsmen kept their promise, gave us their unstinted assistance, and the concert proved to be a great success. The hall was packed to overflowing, and the concert was attended by a number of friends who subsequently participated in the official launching of the Anarchist Red Cross.

I myself first became involved in the Anarchist Red Cross in Philadelphia in 1911. At the time it seemed to me very strange that we should have to found a separate organization. In my hometown in Russia, I remembered we used to collect food and money to help the political prisoners who passed through on their way to Siberia, and we never even thought of asking about their party affiliations. I brought this matter up with several of my comrades, and particularly with one of them named Pade, whose arguments finally convinced me I was wrong.

On this subject I inquired of M. Berezin,[9] who himself escaped from a *katorga* prison and later wrote a book in Yiddish, *From Chains to Freedom*, (published in 1916 by the ARC in New York) in which he described the life of political prisoners in Russia. This is what he said in his reply: "In some prisons there was little distinction made between anarchists, and other political prisoners, but in others the anarchists were refused any help. That is the reason why I organized the Anarchist Red Cross when I came (to Philadelphia)."

As a final document bearing on the reason for the foundation of the Anarchist Red Cross organizations in the United States, I include a quotation from the already-mentioned historical article on the New York ARC. which M. Weitzman wrote, published in the *Freie Arbeiter Stimme* on the 10th of February 1956:

> The most depressing aspect of reports coming was the incredible fact that only Social Democrats seemed to benefit from the aid which was coming from America. Our comrades had raised the funds and gave generously of their own resources to alleviate the desperate plight of all fighters for freedom in Russia.
>
> We began to seek ways and means to arouse public opinion in both Jewish and non-Jewish circles to a realization of the privations, tortures and unspeakable tragedies that had befallen our comrades in Russian prisons and labor camps. To further our aim, we obtained a number of personal letters smuggled out from our deported and captive brethren and submitted them to the editors of a number of local Yiddish and English-speaking newspapers and magazines. However, as soon as the editorial offices learned that Anarchists were involved in the campaign, they began to resort to all kinds of idle pretexts to defer the publication of the stories, and in the end, these reports never saw the light of day.
>
> In order to breach this thick partisan wall of silence and sabotage that had been erected to shut out the story of the ordeal of our tormented comrades in Russia, the local Anarchist Red Cross launched the publication of a monthly periodical under the title of *Die Stimme* (The voice), which addressed

itself to the general public here and urged aid for the imprisoned Anarchists in Russia.[10] This journal appeared half in Yiddish and half in Russian; in its pages we also published a selection of the letters written by our captive and deported comrades. The editor of that publication in its early days was our now deceased comrade, Alexander Zager.

The Anarchist Red Cross made a valuable contribution towards helping a certain number of the imprisoned anarchists to flee from Siberia and subsequently to find asylum abroad. To this very day there are to be found in a number of free countries comrades whom we literally snatched from the jaws of death in Siberia.

It is only lack of space that prevents me from quoting many other sources which would help to show how the foundation of a separate Anarchist relief organization was rendered necessary primarily by the inhumanly sectarian attitude of those Social Democrats who at the same time claimed to have the intention of bringing to an end the unjust society in which we were then living and in which, unfortunately, we still live."

III

RELIEF IN THE USA, 1908–17

When the first nucleus of the Anarchist Red Cross started in Europe around about the beginning of the present century, its activities were largely concentrated in London, where a committee headed by Kropotkin, Cherkesoff, Rocker, and others set about organizing material help for the imprisoned Anarchists in Russia, mostly through collection and donations sent in from all over Europe and the United States.[1] London was well fitted for this function, since it was the center through which the closest connections were maintained with the Anarchists in Russia, and through which news of the situation of our comrades in prison and exile reached the world.

Consequently, when Weinstein and Katzenelebogen organized their first concert in New York in 1908, they had no idea that from the tiny committee they formed for that purpose there would grow up an enormous organization in the United States which would not only collect large sums of money but would also maintain contact with Anarchist prisoners and exiles in Russia and organize the systematic distribution of material help and the manifestation of moral support. In 1909 Chicago followed the example of New York by organizing its own Anarchist Red Cross, and

Philadelphia followed suit in 1911; there was also a small committee in Detroit and Baltimore.[2]

New York was the center that absorbed the greater number of immigrants who arrived from Eastern Europe; many of them were enthusiasts who dreamed of a Russia liberated from the corrupt government of the Tsars, and it was therefore natural that the Anarchist Red Cross should be successful in that city. Very soon after the first concert in 1908, the two pioneer organizers found that they did not have to worry about seeking help. Almost immediately a permanent organization was formed, and up to the time of its liquidation after the Russian Revolution of 1917, the ARC continued to have hundreds of active members in New York.

Its activities rapidly widened, and they centered around an annual gathering known as the Arestantin Ball (Prisoners' Ball), which became so popular an event in immigrant circles that every year a larger hall had to be found to accommodate the people who wished to attend, and even then, hundreds were often turned away because there was no room for them. The mention of the Arestantin Ball arouses vivid recollections of those early days of the ARC. Thousands of gay people, full of vigor and hope, danced all kinds of Russian dances; the hall itself was decorated in the spirit of the event, and, in order to remind the dancers that in faraway Russia and Siberia people were suffering for a cause we all believed in, there would be tableaux in which young men and women would appear dressed in Russian prisoners' garb, with their hands and feet chained and with soldiers and policemen in Russian uniform guarding them. As well as the Arestantin Ball, a summer excursion was organized every year on the Hudson River. These two annual events brought in a considerable sum of money, to which were added the receipts of subscription lists circulated in their spare time by the hard-working young members of the organization, who kept constantly in their minds the thought of their comrades suffering in Russia.[3]

But raising funds was only one part of the ARC's work— and the least complicated part at that. There was a special committee, working in secret, whose duty it was to carry on correspondence with prisoners and exiles in Russia. This had to be done discreetly, for the Tsarist government kept a sharp eye on its victims; in order not to arouse undue suspicion, each member of the committee had a number of prisoners on his correspondence list to whom he would write as if he were a relative; in any other way the letters would not reach their addresses and the prisoners might also have trouble with the authorities. Because of this need for discretion, most of the correspondence committee were men and women who had experience of underground revolutionary work in Russia and who were therefore adept at getting letters to their destinations under the noses of the Russian authorities.

In the article, which we have already quoted, M. Weitzman reports that in order to give comrades in prison news about our movement, the committee adopted the device of inserting letters into the bindings of books sent to prisoners. For a time, this expedient worked, until one day a book aroused suspicion of the authorities in Irkutsk, who took it apart and found the letter enclosed in it. Since it was regarded as a grave offense both to receive clandestine letters and to have connections with the Anarchist Red Cross, the Tsarist authorities set afoot the trial of the prisoners involved, and it looked as though, instead of helping them, their friends in New York had in fact got them in trouble. Through its connections in Russia, the ARC engaged one of the best lawyers in the country to defend the prisoners involved, but before the trial could reach the courts the 1917 Revolution had taken place, and all the political prisoners were set free.

The Philadelphia Anarchist Red Cross was organized by a group of young people who were members of the famous Radical Library. One of them, who I have already mentioned, was M. Berezin, who had only recently come to the United States as a political refugee. Berezin had been fortunate enough to escape from the Artvisky Prison, one of the worst hard labor jails in Siberia, where he had shared a cell with the famous Egor Sazonoff, who in July 1904 assassinated the minister Von Plehve for his brutal treatment of the Russian people. A few years later Sazonoff committed suicide as a protest against the inhuman conditions endured by political prisoners in the hard-labor prisons, and his act made a very deep impression both in Russia and abroad.

In the early winter of 1912, the first Arestantin Ball was held in Philadelphia. As an advertisement, members of the ARC committee attended dances of friendly organizations in the guise of prisoners. When the *Jewish Daily Forward* held its annual masked ball, Berezin suggested that we should create living pictures illustrating the life of the political prisoners undergoing hard labor. His suggestion was accepted, and at the ball we erected a tent with three compartments; in the first was shown the march of political prisoners through the cold Siberian winter towards their place of confinement; in the second was shown the kind of life which each man lived in his cell; in the third was represented the suicide of Egor Sazonoff. When the ball was in full swing, we showed our tableaux, and they made a deep impression on the thousands of dancers who crowded round to watch. Later, when we passed in the Grand March before the judges who were appraising the various fancy dresses, we were accorded the loudest popular applause. However, the judging went in accordance with the saying, "Where there is politics you will not find justice"; it was a Socialist ball, and therefore Anarchists could not get the first prize even if they deserved it; we had to be content with the second prize of $25.

Our own ball, the first Arestantin Ball, was a great moral and financial success, and this was the case during all the ensuing years, so that we were able to collect considerable sums of money to send to the organization in New York.

The Chicago Anarchist Red Cross, organized in 1909, grew rapidly into a large and energetic organization; at the time of its liquidation in 1917 it had 300 members, most of them young people. It became so popular in immigrant circles that every affair organized by it was highly successful, while much money was collected from various Jewish Russian societies, including not only progressive groups, but even religious organizations, which, as soon as they heard that their donations would go to political prisoners in Russia, would often give freely.

The two large annual events organized by the ARC in Chicago were the Bouren Ball (Peasant Ball) on Thanksgiving Day, and the Arestantin Ball in March, both of which were so popular that the older comrades still talk about them with nostalgia.

The Bouren Ball centered around an elaborate caricature of the institution of marriage. Long wires were strung across the hall, from which were suspended various fruits which represented the "forbidden fruit" of the Garden of Eden. Around the hall were booths in which stood members of the organizing committee, dressed as priests of the various religious denominations, as well as girls in peasant dresses and young men in the uniforms of policemen and soldiers. The girls would propose marriage to the men with whom they danced, and when the men refused them, the girls would call upon the policemen or soldiers for help; the men would be arrested and taken before one of the priests, who would perform a ceremony of marriage, give the girl a ring and collect a fee from the man. Afterwards the girl would demand a divorce, and the man would be brought before the judge, who would ask for a second fee for dissolving the marriage. In addition, any man who wished to twist one of the forbidden fruits from its wire would be arrested and fined. These fees and fines brought in most of the proceeds of this event.

Usually, the Bouren Ball would begin at two or three in the afternoon, but it would rarely end before midnight, when the Grand March would begin, led by a giant rooster, followed by the "representatives of the State and of Religion," and then by the girls and boys in peasant costume and the general public, most of them in various kinds of fancy dress. At the end prizes would be given for the most attractive costumes, and also to the girls who had been married and divorced most often during the Ball. After the ARC came to an end in 1917, the Bouren Ball was taken over by the Chicago Workers' Institute and later by the Workmen's Circle, but it never regained the gaiety and meaning it had held for all of us in the early days.

In Chicago, as in New York and Philadelphia, the Arestantin Ball was always a great success. Until 1913 it was only a dance, at which a few members of the committee would dress up as prisoners, but in that year a few members of the Philadelphia group arrived in Chicago, bringing with them the idea of living pictures of prison life in Russia.

At that same time there was a dramatic group among the Russian radicals in Chicago; we invited them to help us, selected a group of actors from our large membership, and, under the direction of Pokatiloff,[4] worked hard at creating our living pictures. In March 1914, we produced them for the first time at the Arestantin Ball, to the astonishment of the guest, many of whom saw—reenacted in the ball-room—the kind of scenes in which they had taken part before leaving Russia. There were representations of street demonstration, fights at the barricades, arrests, political prisoners on the march to Siberia, life in prison, and, at the end, a grand tableau of Hope. This was in the form of a pyramid; at the bottom lay the defeated Tsar, with his brutal police and army officers and priests, on the pyramid itself stood peasants, workers, intellectuals and students, representing the people of Russia with their longing for freedom, and on top was the Statue of Liberty with a torch in her hand—played by a school girl named Emma Avedon whose long blonde hair, spreading over her shoulders, made her portrayal extremely effective. This final tableau made a deep impression; one could see on the faces of those who watched how deeply they were moved by the memory of what they had lived through and by their hopes for a better future in their homeland.

Since it had a similar experience with the local Jewish press as its fellow committee in New York, gaining no publicity for its big annual events in such quarters, the Chicago Anarchist Red Cross decided to publish yearly a humorous bulletin called "The Bouren Ball," which was distributed throughout the Jewish colony in Chicago. We also advertised our events by means of a painter named Goroditsky, who carried his tools about in a horse-[drawn] wagon; we would make two large signs which covered the wagon, and in this way our dances were publicized all over Chicago for months before they actually took place.

In 1915 or 1916 a committee of the Chicago ARC went to Milwaukee and addressed a group of sympathizers there in the hope of setting up a branch in that city. After some discussion it was decided that the Chicago organization would help to organize a Bouren Ball in Milwaukee. However, the interest was not lasting enough for us to be able to create a permanent organization there.[5]

Up to 1913 the money, which was collected in Chicago, was sent to Peter Kropotkin in England, but in that year the distribution of funds was reorganized. The Chicago Anarchist Red Cross came to an understanding with the New York organization, by which the latter sent us a portion of the names of imprisoned Russian Anarchists who were on their lists, and we undertook to help them. After we received the names, a correspondence committee was elected to send material help directly to Russia, and this closer contact with the Russian prisoners made our work much more interesting. At the same time, we had such a large income that we were still able to send money to New York and London, even after fulfilling the responsibilities we had accepted.

At the beginning of this century Detroit did not have a large Russian or Jewish colony, but when the Ford Company announced that they would pay $5.00 a day the immigrants began to move there, and among them was organized the Relief Society for Russian Political Prisoners, to which all the Russian political groupings belonged. The money, which this society collected, was sent to the Russian Political Red Cross, on the assumption that political prisoners of all shades of opinion would receive help from the collective funds.

However, in 1912 and 1913 rumors began to reach Detroit—and they were later confirmed by letters which some Anarchists received from friends in Russian jails—that Anarchist prisoners were receiving no help from the collective fund in the United States, owing to that fact that the Social Democrats had control of it. This news was taken up at the meeting of the Relief Society in Detroit, and for months a bitter fight went on there, until the Anarchists realized that no result favorable to them would come from the dispute. Accordingly, in 1914, they set up a local ARC, which received a good response and was able to send funds both direct to Russia and also to the committee in New York.[6]

IV

THE KERENSKY PERIOD, 1917

It is impossible to forget the winter night in March 1917, when we came out of the Chicago Opera House and heard the newsboys shouting loudly in the lobby: "Revolution in Russia! Tsar Nicholas abdicates!" Each one of us bought a paper, and we rushed into a restaurant where we read every word twice over, and then looked for the news between the lines. We saw that the Romanoff dynasty had come to an end, yet our minds were still full of suspicion, and we could not get used to the idea that our long fight to liberate Russians from the Tsar and his corrupt government had at last been successful. We were skeptical, and the thought that it might be merely an attempt to depose the Tsar which would have no lasting effect. But the next day brought us more and fuller news, and our doubts vanished. The Russian colonies all over the United States began to celebrate, and high-spirited mass meetings were held by every political group. In the joy of the moment, every radical seemed to feel it his duty to attend the functions of other parties and groups, and it was in every way a time of brotherly feeling.

Events in Russia moved very quickly, and soon we received the news that all political prisoners had been set free. In these circumstances the future of the Anarchist Red Cross naturally came up for discussion, and special meetings were held at which the unanimous conclusion was reached that our mission had come to an end and that we should liquidate our organization.

Meanwhile, as soon as the first news of the Russian Revolution reached them, the vast majority of the political refugees then living in the United States thought immediately of returning to help build a new society and to help defend the new freedoms which had been won with so much suffering, but at first these desires seemed far from fulfillment, partly because the great majority had no financial means and partly because of the disruption of transport by the First World War. However, the dream of return came true when Kerensky came into power and the Provisional Government decided that it would pay all the expenses of political refugees and their families returning to Russia.

The first small group, which included L. Trotsky, left very soon; it was detained for a while in Halifax, Canada, but was set free and allowed to go on to Russia as a result of the representation by the Kerensky government.

Soon afterwards a special committee of representatives of all Russian political groupings was formed in New York, and this committee, working in cooperation with the Russian consul, became the clearinghouse for those who were entitled to a free passage home. A similar committee was later formed in Chicago to represent the political refugees in the Midwestern states; in a few weeks it approved several hundred applications, and soon the first group was ready to leave Chicago, accompanied by a contingent from Detroit.

Since the Atlantic was at this time a dangerous ocean to cross, it was decided that all the political refugees would leave from the Pacific coast and go through Siberia to whatever point in Russia they wished to reach.

The departure of the first group from Chicago was a sight never to be forgotten. It seemed as though the whole radical Russian and Jewish colony had come to the station to see their friends go home. Later, during April, May and June 1917, contingents from the eastern states were constantly passing through Chicago and each arrival became the excuse for a celebration.

The first months of the Russian Revolution brought a feeling of brotherhood between the various political groups, but this spirit did not last long. The well-known Bolshevik, Bukharin, came to Chicago to give a few lectures on the Revolution, predicting that a "proletarian" revolution would soon take place in Russia. After his lectures the small Bolshevik group in Chicago began to act as if they would soon take over affairs, and their representatives on the Political Refugee Committee began to claim that they were the only real representatives of the Russian people and that for this reason they alone had the right to decide who could go back to Russia.

Their declaration resulted in a bitter fight, which lasted through one meeting of the committee until past midnight. When the rest of the members saw that it was impossible to reach an understanding with the Marxists, they decided to go to another hall to terminate the business on the agenda. Accordingly, at 3 a.m., all the members of the committee except the Bolsheviks and the Mensheviks went to the Russian IWW hall on Roosevelt Road. The first question discussed there was the election of a special committee, which would go next day to the Russian consul and explain to him what had happened. About 5 a.m. a certain Mr. Berg, later to become famous under the name of Borodin, came to us and proposed that we should not be hasty and should find a way to work with the Bolsheviks. His proposal was not accepted, and we told him to let the Russian consul decide the matter.

Later in the morning, when our committee arrived at the consul's office, the Bolsheviks and Mensheviks were already there. Our chairman and secretary explained what had happened the previous night. The consul was shrewd enough to understand what the Bolsheviks were driving at, and he said that he would acknowledge no new committee and would deal only with our present chairman and secretary, giving passports and money solely on their recommendation. So, in the end, the Bolsheviks had to come to our committee and to accept the common decisions.

When the last group of returning refugees left Chicago in June 1917, the activities of the Anarchist Red Cross seemed to have reached an end; neither those who left for Russia nor those who remained in the United States dreamed that in a few years they would have to organize another Anarchist Red Cross to help the new political prisoners in Russia. We could not foresee that the brutalities of the Tsar's government would seem like child's play in comparison with those which the new despots of Russia would initiate. The whole thinking world imagined that Russia was on the way to becoming one of the most democratic countries in the world.

However, before we come to the new tragedy of Russia it is appropriate to trace the adventures of those who returned in that year of 1917. More than 90 percent of those who went back were later to die in the Bolshevik terror. From some of those who escaped, we have collected information as to their journey back to Russia.

Generally speaking, the travel of the political refugees had been admirably arranged; there were Pullman cars on the trains, second-class accommodation on the boats, and hospitality in the cities. However, when the last group left, the special train was, either through intent or error, formed of old and shabby cars. The refugees refused to board it, but when the railway agent arrived, he claimed that he had no other cars in Chicago and promised that when the train reached St. Paul the next morning the refugees could go to the yards and pick out any cars they might want. This assurance was accepted, and the annoyance was forgotten in the excitement of farewells, for the station was packed with the friends and families of the departing men and women. As the train moved out, the refugees began to sing revolutionary songs, and the people on the platform wept and waved as the wheels of the train seemed to pick up the rhythm of the singing.

Next morning in St. Paul a train of new cars was indeed waiting, and then, as the train began its long journey over the western Canadian prairies, the refugees settled down to consider the realities of their situation, of their return to their country—a country, which for the first time in centuries, was free. At first small groups began to discuss what they could expect to find in this new free Russia, and these private conversations soon developed into mass discussions in which whole cars would take part, and then individuals would wander to other cars where the members of other political groupings were talking, and so, in all this speculation, the journey to Vancouver was hardly noticed.

In Vancouver the Russian consul was waiting for the train. He had made arrangements for hotel accommodations. A large group of other refugees was already there, and two days later the whole contingent crossed to Victoria, on Vancouver Island, and there boarded the liner *Empress of Asia.*

The ten days' voyage across the Pacific was an experience in itself. The whole second-class portion of the ship was occupied by the political refugees so that it looked like a small and very happy Russian community. Among them were many outstanding personalities, including the anarchist writer Volin,[1] whose important book, *The Unknown Revolution*, was published a few years ago, the American writer and artist John Reed, author of *Ten Days That Shook the World*, who was then a follower of Emma Goldman but later became a Bolshevik, William Shatov and many other writers and speakers.[2] As soon as they settled down on the ship an educational committee was elected and, since a mimeograph machine was available, a daily paper was published under the title of *The Float*, which commented on life in the ship's community and contained articles on the Russian Revolution, satirical writing, and many cartoons by John Reed. Volin gave a series of lectures on the history of the Russian revolutionary movement, others spoke on different subjects, and there were musicals and other entertainment, so that the passengers were constantly busy in one way or another and the voyage passed like a dream.

In Yokohama there were already so many returning Russians that the passengers of the *Empress of Asia* had to stay in native Japanese hotels. The reason for this congestion was the relative backwardness of Japanese transportation facilities at this time. There were two ways of getting from Japan to Russia; one was by a short sea trip to Korea, and then by train through Korea and Manchuria, and the other was by small boat to Vladivostok, which involved a longer and usually rough and unpleasant sea voyage. Except for one very small group, everyone decided to go by train, and a party was sent off each day according to the number of tickets that could be obtain from the railroad.

Shortly after the arrival of the party we are following, some unpleasant rumors began to spread in Yokohama about a clash between returning refugees and the Russian authorities in Harbin. What had actually happened nobody knew, but the tale scared a few families who decided to remain for the time being in Japan, and this was the first crack in the holiday spirit with which the party had set out, for now everybody began to think of what they might expect when they reached the Russian border.

The Chicago party crossed the border at a small station where they had to change to a Russian train. Not far from the station the Russian border guards were walking up and down, and some of the returning refugees started a conversation with them. They found out that all the poor soldiers actually knew was that there was no longer a Tsar in Russia; this news they were very happy to impart.

As they approached Harbin, where their train would connect with the main Vladivostok-Moscow line, the refugees began to feel some uncertainty, in view of the rumors they had heard in Japan. They could see the blaze of lights in the station, and then, as the train slowed down, a military band struck up the Marseillaise, and a crowd of people ran towards the carriages. The refugees could not understand what was happening, or for whom the music was playing, but very soon men and women began to crowd into their cars and to embrace them. These first comers introduced themselves as members of the Reception Committee for Political Refugees; afterwards, as they got down from the train, the newcomers were greeted enthusiastically by all the people who had gathered in the station. They were astonished and moved by this reception, which seemed to them a manifestation of the warmth of the Russian people, and of the effects of the great changes that had taken place in their homeland.

Nevertheless, they were still puzzled by the rumors that had circulated in Japan, and on the second day they mentioned these to the Harbin reception committee, who gave the following account of the actual incident. A group of refugees from Pittsburgh, including some rather violent individuals, arrived in the city and demanded that they should be sent immediately to Central Russia. The reception committee explained that before this could happen each of them would have to be checked by a special committee to establish the authenticity of his revolutionary activities in Russia; the main object of this investigation was to detect any former spies or provocateurs from the old Tsarist police who might be trying to return to Russia. The Pittsburgh group refused to agree to this, and went to see the manager of the railroad, who happened to be a former Tsarist general. He refused to give them traveling facilities, but being an old reactionary, he saw an opportunity to stir up the feelings of those who were still against the Revolution, and one evening a group of these people went to the carriage where the Pittsburgh group was living and tried to burn it. The incident could have ended tragically, but fortunately at that moment a train full of sailors from Vladivostok happened to arrive, and they interfered in the matter. After this experience, the Pittsburgh group realized the need for vigilance, submitted to the committee's investigation, and in a few days left Harbin.

While the group which we were following stayed in Harbin they felt already the spirit of renewal that was in the Russian air at the time, and this feeling continued as they traveled on through Siberia towards their various destinations. Everywhere the words "political prisoners" or "refugees" acted like magic, and at every large station committees of young men and women met the trains and provided food and any other help which the travelers might need. Constantly, in this atmosphere of brotherly love, one felt gratitude, which the people showed towards those who had sacrificed their years and their freedom to help the liberation of Russia. In these idyllic early months of the Revolution there appeared among the Russian people that intensity of human feeling towards each other, which occurs rarely—perhaps not more than once in a century—in the history of any people.[3]

In Siberia, where the majority of political prisoners and exiles were concentrated, the news of the Revolution had been received with profound emotion. In the city of Krasnoyarsk, a center from which the Tsarist government used to send exiles to the remote corners of the Siberian wilderness, the governor received the telegram from the Provisional Government in Petrograd, informing him of the change of the regime. He was in no hurry to tell the people of the liberation, but the telegraphist who had received the message passed the news to a few of his friends, and it spread quickly among the resident exiles. Excitement ran high, and in the evening a large deputation went to the city hall to see the mayor and ask him to call on the governor in order to find out the text of the telegram. The people who had gathered outside the city hall were so excited that the mayor decided to take out a copy of the telegram, which had been passed to him, and read it to them. At first the news was so surprising that nobody knew whether to believe it, but after that their joy was unbounded, and all night long the celebrations went on in the streets of the city.

A few days later the exiles began to arrive from the remote places to which they had been banished; they walked as free men in the streets, but there was still fear in their faces, the fear of the dark past from which they emerged. Their clothing was ragged, their shoes were worn-out, and most of them were half-starved, so a committee was organized to take care of them. It had no funds, but here also the new spirit of free Russia was made manifest, for the merchants of the city offered to provide without payment whatever might be needed for the exiles, and even the noblewomen of Krasnoyarsk came to the committee and offered their help.

Yes, a social revolution can produce miracles of brotherhood, and if the political parties which were busily fighting for power had turned their attentions to keeping up these miracles, Russia and the whole world might now be far advanced on the road towards real freedom. Instead, however, we must now consider the bitter reality of what the politics of power actually brought about in Russia.

V

BOLSHEVIK TRIUMPH

The early "honeymoon" months of the Russian Revolution went by happily but all too quickly, as the Russian people, and particularly the Russian peasants, waited for the miracle which they hoped would change completely the life they had endured for more than three centuries under the domination of the Russian Tsars and their feudal governments.

What the Russian people in general expected from the Revolution was the end of hunger and of the bloodshed of the First World War. In addition, the peasants wanted satisfaction of their centuries old dream of possessing the land they worked, while the workers desired the control of industry. The Provisional Government, on the other hand, contained many people who were opposed to any kind of radical change, and in consequence its activities reached a stalemate. Instead of even beginning to solve the burning social questions with which it was faced, it decided to embark on an offensive against the German armies, and the land question was left for the attention of the Constituent Assembly, which was to meet in a year or so.

The tense situation that resulted brought about the first clashes between the revolutionaries and the Provisional Government; as a result, there were political prisoners once again in the new Russia. However, the Provisional Government contained a large proportion of members who were themselves revolutionaries and knew what imprisonment meant, so that there was not yet the cruelty which characterized the Bolsheviks in later years. Those arrested were usually released quickly, and it still seemed as though the spirit of the Revolution were fully alive.

But events moved very quickly during that summer of 1917. The peasants, workers, and soldiers were becoming more and more disappointed with the situation, and the left-wing elements felt that the Revolution was in danger of being brought to a halt. The Bolsheviks, the Left Socialist-Revolutionaries and the Anarchists all continued to agitate for a broadening of the Revolution's scope, and by the early autumn it was evident that new developments were on the way. In October 1917, what everybody had expected took place, the Provisional Government of Kerensky was overthrown, and Russia started on a new social road, a road no country in the world had traveled before, towards a communized system of soviets in which the will of the people would govern from below, instead of the will of the government ruling from above. "All Power to the Soviets," "Workers' Control of Industry," "The Land to the Peasants"—under these magnificent slogans, a new social order seemed to be born in Russia, and it looked as though a real social revolution were taking place. The peasants did not wait for any laws to authorize them to divide the land, and the workers quickly organized shop and factory committees and industrial soviets for the control of places of work. The coalition government of Bolsheviks and Left Socialist-Revolutionaries had to acknowledge these developments by issuing decrees authorizing the taking over of the land and factories, and the construction of the new way of life seemed to be beginning.

Yet the happiness engendered by these events was already tinged with violence and it soon became evident that the Civil War was impending. The Civil War actually started in January 1918; it began with the expedition of the Tsarist General Kornilov in the Kuban region of southern Russia, and it soon spread to other areas. Many of the active revolutionary elements were drawn to the military fronts so as to fight against the counterrevolutionary armies; the Bolsheviks took advantage of this situation to organize their power in Moscow and to start negotiations with the Germans for a separate peace. This move, on their part, led to the withdrawal of the Left Socialist-Revolutionaries from the Coalition Soviet Government. The Socialist-Revolutionaries took matters into their own hands in an attempt to disrupt the peace negotiations, and members of the party shot and killed the German Ambassador Mirbach.

The Bolsheviks were looking for an excuse to loosen their Cheka (secret police) against groups who opposed them, and this assassination gave it to them. All over Russia members of the Left Socialist-Revolutionary Party were arrested, and this resulted in the attempt on Lenin's life by the Socialist-Revolutionary Dora Kaplan.[1] This in turn brought about a wave of cruel reprisals on the part of the Bolsheviks, who this time were not content to attack the Socialist-Revolutionaries, for in April 1918, they staged an armed raid on the Anarchist paper *Anarchy* in Moscow and on the club connected with it. Later, in Leningrad and in the provinces, many Anarchists were arrested, and the Russian prisons started once more to fill with political prisoners.[2]

Actually, from the October Revolution of 1917 to the middle of 1919 most of those arrested were released quickly. The Bolsheviks still seemed to have some kind of moral feeling and many of them did not relish seeing their comrades-in-arms of the October Revolution in prison. They had not yet become accustomed to the cruel terror, which G.P. Maximoff described so vividly in his book, *The Guillotine at Work*.

In September 1919, however, a member of an underground group threw a bomb into a meeting of the Moscow committee of the Bolshevik Party, and this resulted in mass arrests of anarchists all over Russia.[3] In the meantime the widespread Confederation of Anarchist Organizations in the Ukraine, which went by the name of Nabat,[4] also began to feel the effects of the growing reaction in Moscow. Here and there, even at this distance from the capital, Anarchist militants were arrested, and even the Revolutionary Army led by the Anarchist Nestor Makhno began to suffer from the pressure exerted by L. Trotsky, who was anxious to destroy this non-Bolshevik force.

In these circumstances it soon became clear that some kind of organization would have to be created once again to help Anarchists in Russian prisons, and in Moscow, Kharkov, Odessa, and many smaller cities there sprang up organizations, which soon became known as the Black Cross.[5] In the Ukraine and in other parts of Russia where food was easy to obtain it was not hard to help the prisoners, but in Moscow, where food was scarce, the work of these newly formed relief organizations was difficult, although they were helped by Anarchists who came from the Ukraine and always tried to bring food with them;[6] very often however, even this would be confiscated by Bolshevik guards encountered on the way.[7]

Taganka Prison, in Moscow, was the scene of much misery and hardship during those bleak days of civil war. The imprisoned Anarchists, nearly all down with scurvy and many developing pneumatory [*sic*] and heart defects from the unhealthy conditions of their incarceration, addressed a collective appeal on June 3, 1921, to their comrades on the outside. "Without exaggeration," they wrote, "we may say that the imprisonment becomes a slow form of death by starvation." More than just a syllabus of a miserable prison life, the letter from Taganka Prison was, in the words of the prisoners themselves, a plea to their comrades: "redouble your energy, to strain your efforts to the utmost, to coordinate as much as you can the work of the various organizations of the 'Black Cross,' and to inform all those about our starvation who may be in a position to extend effective aid to the 'Black Cross' and the imprisoned comrades."

But it was after the Civil War finally came to an end that the Bolsheviks openly showed their intentions towards any kind of opposition to their dictatorship that might rise up among the Russian people, and the following account of their dealings with the Anarchists at this time is a sufficient illustration of the bad faith with which they behaved.

In order to smash the White Armies of Generals Denikin and Wrangel, the Bolshevik government needed the cooperation of Makhno's Revolutionary Army, which at this time was operating in the rear of Denikin's forces. Accordingly, they sent a delegation to Makhno with the proposal that he should cooperate with the Red Army, and that in return for this the Bolsheviks would guarantee that, after the Whites had been defeated, the anarchist movement would be granted full right of existence in Russia. An agreement on this basis was signed, and one of its main points was that an all-Russian convention of the Anarchist movement should be called in Kharkiv at the end of 1920.

Denikin's army was soon smashed by the combined attacks of Makhno's forces and the Red Army; its survivors fled to the shores of the Black Sea and then to Turkey. Wrangel's army, which was entrenched on the Crimean Peninsula, created a much more difficult problem, since the narrow isthmus which connects the Crimea to the mainland was heavily fortified, and a frontal attack would have been suicidal. Makhno accordingly decided upon a risky maneuver; avoiding the isthmus itself, he sent his men across the tidal flats during the night and in the morning attacked from the rear.

It was the end of the Civil War, but it was also the end of the Bolsheviks' promises and of the agreement that had been signed with Makhno. Trotsky decided to liquidate Makhno's army and did so eventually after many months of bitter fighting, while the Anarchist convention in Kharkov was turned into a trap and most of the delegates who arrived to take part in it were arrested.[8]

In February 1921, the situation worsened as a result of the rebellion of the men of the Baltic Fleet at Kronstadt. This created panic among the Bolsheviks, and after the crushing of the uprising arrests went all over Russia, until the prisons were packed beyond their capacity and the Bolsheviks opened their first Arctic concentration camp in the old monastery on Solovetsky Island. The situation was so bad that the nonpartisan Red Cross Society, headed by Peshkova, and the Anarchist Black Cross had a hard job providing even minimum assistance for the inmates of the Moscow prisons, which were packed with members of every section of the Socialist movement in Russia.[9]

At this time Russia was virtually isolated, and it was almost impossible to let the rest of the world know what was going on there. Furthermore, it seemed at least doubtful whether the free world would believe that political prisoners and exiles were once more a reality in Russia.

However, a break in the situation came in 1921 when a group of Anarchists who were in the Taganka Prison in Moscow decided to declare a hunger strike to the death in protest against the Bolshevik brutalities, and to reinforce a demand for the release of all the political prisoners.[10] At this time, in the hope of enlisting on their side labor organizations throughout the world, the Bolsheviks had organized an International Trade Union Congress in Moscow to which came many delegates from Anarcho-Syndicalist organizations. When the delegates arrived in Moscow the Anarchist Black Cross arranged a meeting with the Anarcho-Syndicalist representatives to inform them of the hunger strike prisoners. At this meeting men and women of international repute, such as Alexander Schapiro, Olga Frydlin, Alexander Berkman and Emma Goldman, gave the Anarcho-Syndicalists from abroad a full report of what was going in Russia and on what the Bolsheviks were doing to all shades of Socialists opinion except their own.[11]

The foreign delegates decided to take up the matter on the floor of the congress, and the next day they did so. The Bolsheviks tried hard to prevent this move, for they were anxious to avoid the news spreading abroad that they had made political prisoners of the men and women who had fought beside them in the October Revolution. Bukharin maintained in the congress that it was untrue that Anarchists were incarcerated; those in prison were, he asserted, "bandits." The fight continued for several days, and in the meantime the hunger strike went into its second week, until the strikers could not walk around their cells and some at least among them seemed very near death.

In these circumstances a committee was organized from among those attending the congress for the purpose of making representations to Dzerzhinsky, who was then head of the Cheka, and to Lenin. With Dzerzhinsky the delegation had a bitter discussion, but they could get no satisfaction from him. Lenin first refused to see them, but they sent a message that they would stay at the gates of the Kremlin until they were admitted. Eventually, knowing that the men standing outside in that cold winter night included not only Anarcho-Syndicalists, but also independent labor leaders like Tom Mann from England, he changed his mind. However, when he did see the delegates, he repeated Bukharin's statement that the arrested Anarchists were dangerous bandits who could not and should not be released. The delegation insisted on a more satisfactory answer, and Lenin promised that they would discuss the matter with Trotsky, Bukharin, Zinoviev, and Kamenev, and would send a definite answer the next day.

This answer came in the form of a letter from Trotsky, who wrote in the name of the Central Committee of the Communist Party. He claimed that the delegation had not been fully informed about the situation and repeated once again the story about the prisoners being bandits. However, in conclusion he stated that the Communist Central Committee had decided that, if the hunger strikers were willing, they should be deported from Russia. The strikers accepted this condition, and soon afterwards they were released from prison; after many weeks of uncertainty, they were deported and traveled with their wives, under extremely miserable conditions, to Berlin. Their departure gave at least a ray of hope that the rest of the world would at last get to know what was going on in Russia, and that somehow help might reach the Anarchists who still remained in prison and exile.

Within Russia itself the situation became steadily worse. The Bolsheviks had evidently decided to liquidate every kind of opposition to their ruthless dictatorship. Arrests continued in every part of Russia, until they took on the proportions of a mass hunt directed against all opposition sections of the Socialist movement. Those who for the time being were fortunate enough to be left alone did their utmost to help those in need.

In particular, the All-Russian Black Cross sent out an appeal to all parts of the country for help. At this time the food situation in Russia was so bad that almost everybody was half-starving, but the comrades who were at large did everything they could to get supplies to those in prison. Even more difficult than collecting food was the task of getting it to those who needed it. In the cities, indeed, it could be taken to the prisoners as presents from their families, and this did not involve any great risk. But to reach those in concentration camps and particularly on Solovetsky Island raised much greater problems. Neither the post office nor the railways were functioning properly at this time, and the only moderately sure way of getting help to detainees in such places was for comrades to travel there. Apart from the hardship of the journey itself, this involved great risks to the messenger's own freedom. There were many occasions when Anarchists returning from trips to concentration camps were arrested.[12] It was a desperate and dangerous time for all those who wished to help the new generation of political prisoners.

The end of 1921 brought at least some cause for hope. A Congress of the Anarcho-Syndicalist International was organized in Berlin. The German organizers knew already that Emma Goldman, Alexander Berkman, and Alexander Schapiro were anxious to leave Russia, so they wrote requesting their presence at the meetings of the Congress. The three of them applied for passports, and since at this time the Bolsheviks were anxious to gain the sympathy of European workers' organizations, their request was granted. Very soon they were out of the reach of the Communist dictatorship, and as soon as they reached Germany, they issued an appeal to all freedom-loving people to help the political prisoners and exiles in Russia.

Appeal for Help

Having now left Russia, we realize that our first and most necessary statements should be made on behalf of the political prisoners of Russia. It is a sad and heartbreaking commentary upon the state of affairs in Russia if one has to speak about political prisoners in the country of Social Revolution. Unfortunately, such is the actual state of things.

And by political prisoners we do not refer to the counter-revolutionists who are the prisoners of the Revolution. Unbelievable as it may seem, the prisons and jails of Soviet Russia are now crowded with the revolutionary elements of the country: men and women of the highest caliber, of the highest social ideals and aspirations. Throughout the vast expanses of the country, in Central Russia and in Siberia, in the prisons of the old and new regime, in the solitary cells of the Cheka, revolutionists of all parties and movements are now languishing: Left Social-Revolutionist, Maximalists, Communists from the "workers' opposition," Anarchists, Anarcho-Syndicalist, and Universalists—Partisans of various schools of social philosophy, but all true revolutionists and active participants of the November Revolution of 1917. The situation of the political prisoners is highly deplorable. Apart from moral sufferings and torments, the purely physical side of their existence is extremely lamentable. Due to the general state of the country, the lack of building materials and skilled workers, alterations of prisons have become nearly nigh impossible. That is why the hygienic conditions in most of the prisons are now of the most primitive kind. But worse than all, is the food problem. At no time did the Bolshevik government supply its prisoners with sufficient food. The rations given to prisoners fell upon their friends, relatives, and comrades. But now the situation has taken a turn for the worse. Only 52 percent of the food tax collections have thus far been taken in. With famine conditions now existing in the Volga provinces, with the general breakdown of the economic apparatus of the government, the situation of the prison population has indeed become hopeless.

The needs of the political prisoners are satisfied, of course by the Political Red Cross, a faithful and active organization. One of the outstanding members of this organization is the eminent revolutionist, Vera Figner. This organization was very successful in its mission considering how difficult it is for anyone to save anything from one's meager ration. However, the Political Red Cross until now has been able to supply the most basic needs of the political prisoners. Of all the prisoners with the exception of the Anarchists! Not because the Red Cross is discriminatory in its work. Just the opposite—the organization is nonpartisan in its work, although strongly colored by the rightist convictions of the Socialist elements. But, guided by political reasons, the Anarchists of Russia have always reverted to self-aid in the work of helping the imprisoned comrades, for the purpose of which an Anarchist Red Cross (now called the Black Cross) was set up with the aim of providing for the Anarchists in the Russian prisons. This has now become a Herculean task for the Anarchists who still happen to enjoy their freedom. Many of the most active comrades have given their life for the Revolution, while others were executed or thrown into the Bolshevik prisons. Many of those who survived and are still at liberty are themselves on the very brink of starvation: the Black Cross has to make superhuman efforts to keep the political prisoners from starving to death. The work done by it is one of self-sacrifice and high nobility.

But if its work was always hard and full of obstacles it has become immeasurably more difficult. The new policy of systematic persecutions of Anarchists by the Bolshevik government is the greatest obstacle in the work of the Black Cross. Since most of its members have been imprisoned by now, the organization was revamped and now it is known under the name of the Society to Aid Anarchist Prisoners in Russia. It heroically continues the work of extending to the prisoners the small material aid, which it succeeds in collecting. Unfortunately, its possibilities to do so are very limited. The comrades who are at liberty deprive themselves from the basic necessities in order to send a few pounds of bread or potatoes to the prison. They are eager to share the last they have. But they themselves have so little, and the number of comrades in prison is so vast and their need so great! From the prisons of Moscow, Petrograd, Orel, and Vladimir, from the far-off eastern provinces, from the comrades exiled to the frozen north, from everywhere comes that frightful news: the terrible whip of famine, the dreadful scurvy. Their hands and feet swell up, their gums weaken, their teeth are falling out. Their bodies are actually disintegrating.

Comrades who are at liberty, pay heed to this cry for help! The Anarchists in Russia cannot supply the barest need of the imprisoned comrades unless helped in this work by the comrades abroad. In the name of the Society to Aid Anarchist Prisoners in Russia, in the Bolshevik prisons, who suffer now for their faithfulness to the highest ideals, in the name of all of them, we call upon you, comrades and friends, from everywhere. Only your voluntary and immediate aid will be able to save our imprisoned comrades of Russia from starving to Death.

With comradely greetings,

Alexander Berkman
Delegate at large from the
Society to Aid Anarchist Prisoners in Russia[13]
Emma Goldman and A. Shapiro

VI

THE PALMER RAIDS

Before I go on to tell what was done to help the new generation of political prisoners in Russia, I would like to remind my readers that Russia was not the only country with such prisoners.

Between 1918 and 1924 an organization known as the Political Prisoners' Defense Committee was active in the United States. The political prisoners whom it was called upon to assist were not the victims of either Tsarist or Bolshevik oppression, but the victims of mass hysteria engendered in the minds of the ruling class. The strong protests in the Unites States against conscription, the sympathy aroused among American workers and intellectuals for the Russian Revolution, the widespread labor disputes toward the end of the war, of which the famous General Strike in Seattle was the most dramatic example, caused great anxiety in government circles in Washington and resulted in the infamous "Palmer Raids."

During the past year the press, radio, and television in this country have been busy telling the American people about the Russian atrocities in Hungary, and they were completely justified in their condemnation of the Communist action, but, lest we forget, let us remind the

American people of the brutal mistreatment to a small minority of radical dissenters in the freedom-loving United States, of the ruthless police raids, imprisonment and deportation, during the reign of terror of Attorney General Palmer. Cruelty and oppression are to be condemned, no matter who inflicts it, and we cannot blind ourselves to our past. Those who experience the misery and anxiety of the Palmer Raids certainly cannot forget them, and they will remain a stigma that is difficult to eradicate.

Hilda Kover, one of the active members of the Political Prisoners' Defense and Relief Committee has furnished me with a general statement of the work of the committee. It should be emphasized that this organization was completely separate from the Anarchist Red Cross or any of the groups that succeeded it, since its work was to give relief to American rather than Russian prisoners.

I. Historical Sketch of the Political Prisoners' Defense and Relief Committee.

The Political Prisoners' Defense and Relief Committee was organized in August 1918, because there was no organization at the time to render aid to those who were being arrested for voicing their opinions on the conduct of war, on our relations with the then-revolutionary government of Russia, or on other unpopular causes. During its existence it supplied many unknown rebels with funds, aided them with getting attorneys, and provided medical help, when necessary.

Among its activities was that of regularly sending packages, money and other necessities to the prisoners. The monthly expenses for relief were often as high as $400, and at one time reached $500.

The people who constituted this committee were working men and women. No salaries were paid to anyone, all work being done voluntarily after their days toil at their respective trades. The cases they handled were usually such as were neglected by other existing organizations. They extended relief to all political prisoners who were in need of it, regardless of their political opinions. The committee also engaged attorneys to take up individual cases with a view to release from prison, which was sometimes granted only on the condition of accepting deportation.

The funds for this work were raised by the committee through personal appeals to various labor and fraternal organizations, by individual collections with subscription lists, and by benefits performances. At one time a noted violinist gave a recital at one of New York's most famous concert halls, and this netted about $1,500. The committee also printed a journal containing letters from the political prisoners receiving its aid, and the sale of this publication was another way of raising funds. No effort, indeed, was too great for the members of the committee to undertake in order to get the necessary funds with which to carry out their work.

In later years other organizations were formed to do the work "systematically," as they called it, with paid officers, office help, overhead expenses, etc. And though some of these organizations claimed to send help to all concerned without any discrimination, the evidence is not conclusive that any such organization at that time did the work in exactly the same manner as the Political Prisoners' Defense and Relief Committee. It was the belief of the members of that committee that because the work was done on the basis of individual rather than organizational contact, the political prisoners who benefited through it had the feeling that a real friend was interested in them—in their little personal problems as well as in the larger one getting relief and ultimate release from prison.

By the end of 1924, after most of the political prisoners—victims of the war-hysteria of 1917–18—were released and even some of the labor prisoners who had been in jails since long before the war were at liberty, the committee was dissolved, since its activities were no longer needed.

II. Statement of the Political Prisoners' Defense and Relief Committee, made in January 1922 to explain the reason for its existence.

Sometime after the Political Prisoners' Defense and Relief Committee came into existence, other organizations, larger in scope, carrying on the work on a national scale, had begun to function, in consequence of which the committee found it necessary to issue the following statement:

Time and again we are being confronted with the question, "Why so many organizations of the same kind?"

It is our desire to answer as follows:

1. Our organization is not of "the same kind." The work we are doing is not conducted by any other organization, i.e., no other organization is carrying

on regular systematic relief work on behalf of the political prisoners in need, without any discrimination as to what party they may or may not belong to. What we do is: send every month a stated sum to each prisoner on our list, also packages of food and other necessities to those who are inmates of prisons where such are allowed. It is our belief that they need this the year round, and not at Christmas time only. While it is true that our organizations are sending occasional relief to some political prisoners, we must repeat that ours is a regular systematic relief. As to our defense work—the cases we take up are such as have been forgotten and neglected, or such as no other organization cared to conduct.

2. It is the opinion of every member of the committee that work of this nature must be conducted on a voluntary basis—everyone giving his time to it outside of his daily work—and that every penny collected on behalf of the political prisoners must be used for them, eliminating overhead expenses of salaries, rents, and so on. And it is because of this that our activities mean so much to the prisoners; we establish a personal relation with each one of our correspondents, and the money we send comes as from friend to friend, and not as from a secretary of an organization, whose duty it is to write to the prisoners. The prisoner feels that the one who writes to him is interested in his health, his well-being, his troubles, and therefore our letters bring cheer and joy to him.

Those documents are self-explanatory, but it will have become evident in reading them that the Political Prisoners'

Defense and Relief Committee, like other organizations about which I write in this booklet, was fighting against the tendency which has been evident in the Left for the past half-century for relief organizations, particularly those dominated by Social Democrats, to become partisan and to give very little help to the individual sufferer who falls outside their particular circle of opinion.

During the period of the Palmer Raids some other, smaller groups attempted to provide nonpartisan assistance to those who suffered from political persecution. One of these appeared as a consequence of the arrival of political prisoners at Leavenworth Federal Prison, beginning in 1918. Owing to the initiative of Bessie Zeglin, a group of women in Kansas City, Missouri, organized a fund for their assistance. Since few of the women belonged to any political movement, and since they did not wish to draw undue attention from the authorities, they called themselves the Women's Tea Club. While there remained any political prisoners in Leavenworth, they continued to be active in providing food, clothing, money, etc., and they gave this help without ever asking to what political group any particular prisoner might happen to belong to.

VII

REVIVAL OF RELIEF IN THE USA, 1921–39

To return to the political prisoners in Russia. After the arrival of the deported Russian Anarchists in Berlin at the end of 1921 and the launching of an appeal there by Alexander Berkman, Emma Goldman, and Alexander Schapiro, the activity of collecting relief funds for political prisoners in Russia began all over again in Western Europe and the United States.

The first step was the organization, by Left Socialist-Revolutionaries and Anarchists, of the Joint Committee for the Defense of the Revolutionaries Imprisoned in Russia. Apart from its work of collecting funds for those in prison, this committee published a regular bulletin, which gave full information on conditions in Russian prisons and places of exile, documented in many cases by letters received from prisoners.

In 1926 this joint committee was dissolved, and the relief work was taken over by the International Working Men's Association (the Anarcho-Syndicalist International), which set up in Berlin a Relief Fund of the IWMA for Anarchists and Anarcho-Syndicalists Imprisoned or Exiled in Russia. Rudolf Rocker, as secretary of the fund, published a regular bulletin giving all the news that was available on the political prisoners and their life in Russia. The fund was supported partly by contributions from the relief committees in various parts of Europe and the United States, and partly from voluntary levies among the members of Syndicalist organizations.

At this time the Bolshevik government did not make very great difficulties about prisoners receiving mail, money, or packages from abroad, and the committee of the relief fund organized a regular correspondence with arrested Anarchists in Russia, and supplied them with cash, food, and clothing, as well as books of various kinds, particularly dictionaries, since many of them had taken up the study of languages in order to pass their time. Every day the work of the relief became heavier, since the Bolsheviks arrested every oppositionist on whom they could lay their hands, and even went so far as to imprison people who had been inactive for years in the Anarchist movement, merely because of their activities in the past.

One of the factors that hampered the work for relief committees in Europe was the economic aftermath of the First World War; inflations, followed by depression, made it difficult to collect adequate funds in European countries to help the prisoners in Russia, and once again, as before the war, the United States became the principal source of material assistance. After receiving an appeal for help from Berkman, Emma Goldman, and Schapiro in 1922, the Anarchists in the United States organized the Anarchist Red Cross Society, which explained its reasons for reappearance in the following statement.[1]

The Anarchist Red Cross, which liquidated its organization in 1917, is being reorganized because of the following circumstances: It is true that the

Revolution of 1917 freed the imprisoned and exiled
Russian anarchists and as a result we suspended the
activities of the Red Cross. But conditions in Russia
have changed for the worse. Men and women are
again arrested and exiled, not only anarchists and
Right Socialists but moderate liberals are also being
persecuted.... And not only in Russia alone does
this situation exist. In France, Italy, Spain, etc., our
comrades are languishing behind iron bars. Our aim
is to help them all as much as possible.

At first it was feasible to form an Anarchist Red Cross
only in New York;[2] and there are several reasons for the
failure of similar groups to spring up immediately in other
American cities. First, the patriotic hysteria of the war
years and the reactionary sentiment of the period of the
Palmer Raids had left a deep impression on those who
had suffered discrimination. Secondly, many people felt a
strong emotional disinclination to believe that their dream
of a free Russia had been destroyed; many of them were
misled by the Bolshevik propaganda and left the movement, while others eventually became so disillusioned that
they ceased to be active. These facts hampered greatly the
organization of relief work and made it difficult to organize
the Anarchist Red Cross on the same scale as before the
Russian Revolution of 1917.

At the end of 1923, when a few comrades returned
to Chicago from a visit to Russia and brought with them
the news of what they had seen there and especially of the
conditions under which the political prisoners and exiles
were living, these negative factors were so strong that it took
very great efforts to collect even a small number of people
to form the Free Society Group in that city, dedicated to

exposing the development of state capitalism in Russia and to raising funds for helping the political prisoners there. With such a small membership it was impossible to organize events like the great balls of prewar years, and at first, we had to concentrate on collecting money by means of small gatherings and through subscription lists and individual donations towards the relief find.

At this time, however, there were a few Russian Social Democrats in Chicago who also were trying very hard to raise money for their political prisoners in Russia. They were on terms of personal friendship with some members of the Free Society Group and used to attend our gatherings. In 1924 one of them suggested that, since both our groups were small and since we both represent movements persecuted by the Bolsheviks, we should combine in the work of raising funds. It seemed a logical proposal, particularly at a time when the Bolsheviks and their fellow travelers were so hostile to anyone who tried to tell the truth about what was happening in Russia. On the other hand, we were reminded of the experiences of Anarchists in Russian prisons where the Social Democrats had refused to give them any help. However, our personal friendship for the individuals who approached us, and a feeling that what had taken place in Russia might have changed their attitude towards the Anarchists, made us agree to their proposal of cooperation, and together we organized a Russian Political Relief Committee.

In the winter of 1924 this committee organized its first large ball in the Workmen's Circle Labor Lyceum.[3] We were all pessimistic, since this was the first considerable gathering among Chicago radicals openly opposed to the dictatorship in Russia; many of us feared that the Bolsheviks would cause trouble, as at this period they did at almost every lecture or meeting in the United States that was critical of the regime in Russia. We need not have been apprehensive; more than a thousand people attended, and their attitude made it, not merely a ball, but also the first mass demonstration so far as Chicago was concerned since the Revolution of 1917, reflecting a mounting feeling of solidarity with those who were once again suffering in the prisons and places of exile. The profits of the ball were equally divided, and the Anarchist and Social Democratic groups each sent its share to the political prisoners in which it was interested. In 1925 we held a second and equally successful ball, but shortly afterwards the more active of our Social Democratic associates left for Los Angeles and those who remained broke off connection with us, so that once again we started work independently as the Chicago Aid Fund.

At this time, since we had collected a considerable sum of money through our balls and other activities, we came to an understanding with the committee in Berlin by which we in Chicago would take over a list of prisoners in Russia and send help directly to them. We organized this assistance as we had done in the days of the original prewar Anarchist Relief Committee, and the direct contact, which we established with prisoners in Russia, aroused a steadily increasing interest in our work.

About 1926 the Anarchist Red Cross in New York liquidated its activities, and we in Chicago remained the only group working regularly at the collection of funds for political prisoners. It is true that the Jewish Federation in New York and some of its individual groups occasionally collected money for the relief fund in Berlin, but it had no constructive and systematic everyday policy on this question; at the same time, it performed a useful function, since it provided a means of establishing contact with non-anarchist Jewish groups, such as the Workmen's Circle branches and some trade unions groups.[4]

Apart from raising funds, it seemed to us even more important that we should carry on propaganda, which would bring to people the real news of the treatment of political prisoners in Russia. In 1925, thanks largely to the initiative of Alexander Berkman, a book entitled *Letters from Russian Prisons* was published in New York by Albert & Charles Boni and had some influence on public opinion. A year later the Chicago Aid Fund decided to expand its work for the relief of prisoners in Russia from a local to a national scale, and, after compiling a considerable mailing list, we began to send our yearly appeals and also bulletins containing news and letters from Russian political detainees. This work brought good results, since it reached out to many towns in the United States where people were still ignorant of what was really going on in Russia.

At the same time, our expansion into national activity aroused a certain amount of antagonism. Some of the groups belonging to the Jewish Federation believed we were trespassing on an area where we had no right to be, and they suggested that all work on a national scale should be done under the direction of the Federation. Joseph Cohen in his book, *The Jewish Anarchist Movement in the United States*, which was published in 1945 by the Radical Library in Philadelphia, has this to say about the Chicago Aid Fund and the jurisdictional fight that occurred in connection with it:

> In Chicago, B. Yelensky organized a separate activity. Yelensky, with the help of Comrade Maximoff and

other Russians, succeeded in establishing direct contact with the imprisoned comrades in Russia, and in developing in the United States a wide and systematic activity, which brought good results. But the jurisdictional fight in connection with it was not at all pleasant, and this question was for long a subject of discussion in the Jewish groups and in the pages of the *Freie Arbeiter Stimme*. In 1927 the Detroit group brought in a recommendation that every large affair or other activity should be organized through the Federation. This recommendation, made without due consideration was thought by the majority of the Jewish comrades to be practical, but it did not bring any practical results.

The reason why we in Chicago opposed the recommendation that the Federation should have jurisdiction over the Aid Fund were two-fold. First, the Federation and its affiliated groups had shown very little interest in the organization of a relief fund on a national scale. Secondly, we considered that from a practical point of view the work of any Red Cross organization must be independent of any propagandists group or Federation. For this reason, in the years before the 1917 Revolution in Russia, the Anarchist Red Cross had been a separate organization, with no leaning towards any particular grouping in the Anarchist movement. The main object of such relief organizations should be to help any Anarchist in prison or in exile, and for this reason we could not accept a recommendation that would place our work under the direction of the Jewish Federation.

Instead of becoming too much involved in this squabble over jurisdiction, the Chicago Aid Fund devoted itself to increasing the scope of its work. The news we received from Russia showed that the situation there, far from improving, was growing steadily worse; very few Anarchists were out of confinement, and concentration camps were being established in Siberia once again, so that it became increasingly difficult to keep in touch with our comrades. Moreover, the Bolshevik authorities were harder to fool with underground schemes that their Tsarist predecessors had been, because they themselves had experienced underground work and they knew virtually every trick that could be tried. Nevertheless, we did our best, not only to send material help to the prisoners, but also, occasionally, to smuggle to them some news of the free world.

Fortunately, as the need for relief increased, so did the response to our appeals, and among the organizations, which helped us were the following:

Russian Groups in New York, Los Angeles, Akron, Youngstown, Gary, East Akron, Philadelphia, Cleveland, Boston, Baltimore, New Haven, San Francisco, Bethlehem, Waterbury, and Dobbs Ferry.

Jewish Groups in Los Angeles, Detroit, and St. Louis, as well as the Radical Library of Philadelphia and the Free Society Group in Toronto, Canada.

English-speaking groups as follows: Freedom Group of New York, Mohegan Colony Group, Stelton Group, Libertarian Group of Los Angeles,[5] Sunrise Colony Group in Michigan, International Group to Help Political Prisoners in Cleveland, Ohio, the Proletarian Group in New York. Also, Spanish and Italian Groups, and the Italian-language newspaper *L'Adunata*.

Apart from the Anarchist movement itself, many branches of the Workmen's Circle responded consistently to our appeals, and at the convocations of this organization our work was endorsed, and recommendations were made that donations should be granted. We were also supported by many locals of the ILGWU, and in our later years this union also supported us at its annual convention.[6] The response of individuals was warm and good and though, as a minority movement, we never collected sensational sums of money, we were satisfied with the results we attained and with the fact that we were able, not only to help the prisoners, but also to keep in the minds of many people the conditions under which political prisoners were living in Russia.

In this latter connection I come now to one of the principal achievements of the Chicago Aid Fund, the publication of the volume entitled, *The Guillotine at Work: Twenty Years of Terror in Russia*, a contribution to the truth about the Bolshevik Terror which historians of the future will doubtless recognize as one of the strongest indictments published in our age of the barbarism committed by the Communists in Russia.

The idea of this book originated in 1935, when Alexander Berkman wrote to Chicago suggesting that, since 1936 would be the fifteenth anniversary of the reestablishment of aid funds for political prisoners in Russia, we might publish a booklet acquainting the American public with the plight of the Russian political prisoners. This suggestion was accepted, as well as another suggestion by Berkman that a committee of three should be selected to carry out the work. G.P. Maximoff, Mark, and the present writer were nominated, and we all agreed to undertake the work.[7] We began by considering what material we should select, since it seemed to us that as things stood, we should not be able to collect enough money to publish anything more than a fairly large pamphlet.

Mark soon left the committee, and Maximoff and I left town. We decided to divide the work according to function, I would be responsible for collecting publication funds and Maximoff would compile and edit the material which was to go into the booklet. The very abundance of his archives on Russia made the task of selection difficult, but soon he had assembled enough material for a work of about 150 pages. However, when we read it over, we realized that this was not really sufficient to give a full picture of what was going on in Russia, so, as our appeal had already brought in a few hundred dollars, we decided to take a risk and expand our pamphlet into a small book. With every few dollars that came in, our plans grew, until in the end we had produced a large volume of 624 pages. Then we had to face the problem of translation into English if the book were to reach a wide audience. Here however, we were fortunate in finding a friend in New York who became interested in our task, and, though we had to pay him a certain amount for his work, since he was penniless at the time, the English version was produced at relatively little expense.

We had planned to get the book ready for publication in 1937, but the outbreak of the Spanish Civil War in 1936 slowed down our work, and it was only in 1940 that *The Guillotine at Work* eventually came off the press. There were many times when I doubted whether we should ever see it completed, and when it did appear the atmosphere was not exactly propitious, since by this time Russia was already at war with Germany and people who only yesterday had been extremely bitter against the Bolsheviks were now inclined to forget the realities of life in Russia. Even some of our own people felt that this was not the right time for the book to be published, but we did not pay any attention to their arguments.

When *The Guillotine at Work* did eventually appear we gained, in compensation for our hard work, the satisfaction of seeing its importance acknowledged by the radical and liberal press. Perhaps because it spoke of the suffering of Anarchists, it did not receive much publicity from the mass newspapers, but even without this it made its way to become one of the important source books on contemporary Russia. Many writers, both with and without acknowledgement, were later to use the information, which we first presented. Apart from reviews in periodicals, we received many letters of appreciation from people who were often unconnected with the Anarchist movement. Among them was the English writer, Herbert Read, who remarked of *The Guillotine at Work* that "it is an overwhelming indictment of the Russian terror and a historical document of the greatest value." By now the book is available in universities and city libraries throughout world.

Meanwhile, in the beginning of 1935, we began to notice that the situation in Russia was taking a sharper turn for the worse than ever before. Registered letters, which we sent to political prisoners, began to come back, with the remark that the address "could not be located," and money we sent would be returned by banks with the advice that they had been unable to deliver it. Furthermore, some of our correspondents began to tell us, in a code we had established with them, of prisoners who had vanished so completely that neither their friends nor their families had any trace of them. Reading between the lines of the letters that got through to us, we realized that the future for political prisoners in Russia was rapidly darkening.

Then came the infamous events of 1936; the Bolsheviks Old Guard was liquidated, and in the persecution that followed all the opposition elements that survived were subjected to the new terror. Finally, in 1939, every contact with our comrades in Russia was broken, and our work for the political prisoners in that country came to an end.[8] After the Second War we managed to establish contact with a comrade who had survived the purges, and also with the family of another comrade which had been brought to Germany by the Nazis; from them we heard that all the Anarchist political prisoners in Russia had disappeared, and that nobody knew when or where they had died at the hands of the brutal forces of State Socialism.

Already in 1936, our contacts with Russia were so sharply reduced that the members of the Chicago Aid Fund began to discuss what should happen to our activities. Some of us hoped that soon our contact with Russian political prisoners might be reestablished, and for this reason we decided to postpone liquidation. Then, in June 1936, we received the tragic news that, after a long illness, Alexander Berkman had taken his own life so that he should not become a burden on his friends. To commemorate his life and work, we decided to rename our organization the Alexander Berkman Aid Fund and to give it an international scope so that we could bring help to political prisoners, not only in Russia, but all over the world.[9]

We did not have to wait long for an opportunity to start our activities on the new basis. In July 1936, the Civil War began in Spain, and the events of that time are well enough known for it to be unnecessary for me to enlarge on them except in so far as they affected the work of our fund.

One of the members of our committee, Maximilian Olay, was well known among the Spanish Anarchists, not only in the United States, but also in Spain itself, and at the beginning of the Civil War he was asked by the CNT and the FAI to supervise their publicity work in North America.[10] The Alexander Berkman Aid Fund decided to take part in this work of putting forward the true aims of the Spanish people and also to undertake the collection of funds to assist Spaniards who might be in need as a result of the Civil War.

By now our own mailing list was a large one, and we obtained many addresses from other groups and organizations, so that we were able to disseminate many thousands of leaflets and other literature, as well as organizing large public meetings, lectures, and film shows to familiarize the public with the true situation in Spain. By these and other means we collected thousands of dollars, which we sent to the help of needy people in Spain.

When resistance to Franco came to an end in 1939 and the supporters of the Republic were evacuated to France and North Africa, we continued our work by collecting funds to help the Spanish refugees, and in this task we collaborated with the SIA (International Anti-Fascist Solidarity), which was organized by the CNT and the FAI in every country where an Anarchist movement existed.[11] The aims of the SIA were similar to those of the Anarchist Red Cross, but it was involved mostly in helping the tens of thousands of refugees who had left Spain, often accompanied by their families. In every American city where there were Spanish radicals the SIA went to work, and it became a very lively organization in which men, women, and children took an active part. But though its gatherings were for a time very popular, even among people who were not themselves Anarchists, it gradually declined as the years went on since Franco's triumph.

VIII

THE SECOND WORLD WAR

The scheming of American and European capitalists, who encouraged the resurrection of the German Junker class and the rise of Hitler as a counterpoise to the Bolsheviks, became like a monstrous boomerang when, in September 1939, the sound of German guns attacking Poland initiated a new chapter in man's history, a chapter of cruelty and inhumanity practiced not merely by the German armies, but also by those self-styled humanitarians who were so extreme in the condemnation of the Germans. As soon as the war began, we realized that we should have an enormous task on our hands, for now it would no longer be a question of helping Russians or Spaniards only, but assisting any victim we could reach.

During this period, we found ourselves almost the only organization able to undertake activity on anything like a large scale. The SIA had more than enough to do in connection with Spanish refugees, and though an International Aid Fund (Interaid) had been organized by the Jewish Federation in New York during 1925, this was intended to aid old people and its activities were therefore somewhat limited.

The work of the Relief Fund, which up to that time had continued to be centered in Berlin, was disrupted by

Hitler's rise to power in 1933; its activity was then transferred for a short time to Holland and later to Paris, where Alexander Berkman reorganized it as the International Working Men's Association Russia Aid Fund. In this form it continued its work and published its regular bulletin until the Nazis invaded France in 1940. Now the work, which it had carried on, fell on American shoulders.

The situation at this time was tense and difficult. The terrible events that were taking place, and particularly such happenings as the pact between Russia and Germany and the German atrocities against the Jewish people, made many of our comrades feel that the ground was melting away under their feet, but we of the Alexander Berkman Aid Fund realized the magnitude of the task before us and the fact that it had to be done in a hurry. We had a few hundred dollars in our treasury, and with this we started to send out help wherever we could.

In the meantime, the first agonizing reports from our comrades in Europe began to reach us; the following letter, which is typical of many, came from Sam Frydman,[1] who had been a political refugee in the United States during the First World War, had returned to Russia in 1917, and had escaped to Paris in 1923, disillusioned with what he saw the Bolsheviks doing to their opponents.

Paris, Sept. 21, 1939

Dear and beloved Boris and Bessie:

It is a long time since we have had employment. I shall probably have to leave in the near future. Dora and Michelle will remain without any means of subsistence, because their means of livelihood became exhausted some time ago.

Michelle is four years old, and very delicate; attached to her mother. Hence it is impossible at this time to place her anywhere else, so that Dora should be able to go to work; the child must stay with her. And it is not yet certain whether they will be allowed to remain in Paris. It is precisely on this account that I want to write to you and to make a request. I have never turned to the movement for any help for myself—for others, yes; and I realize fully your economic situation.

Nevertheless, I beg you, if you can do anything for the family, don't let Dora and the child become destitute. Do everything possible ... to help Dora and the child in such an emergency. You surely understand that without me Dora is helpless; but let us hope that everything will turn out for the best in the end. If you are able to send anything, it is best to handle it through the bank or through the American Express, in Dora's name. On the papers her name appears not as Dora. but as Deborah. If she is not in Paris it will be forwarded to her. This letter is being written by me, not in the name of the movement, but in my own name. The other comrades will probably write their own account.

But you surely understand that it is most urgent to give help to a mother and her child. I hope you will comply with my request. Write, dear friends, all about yourselves and the relatives. Keep in good health, dear and beloved friends Boris and Bessie and the rest.

Sam Frydman

This letter was the last we received; Sam and Dora Frydman lost their lives as Jews somewhere in the German concentration camps, though their daughter was saved by French friends.

With the German occupation of a large part of France in 1940, and the establishment of the Vichy government in the remaining section of the country, the situation of radicals, and particularly of those who were Jewish, became daily more dangerous, and the radical movements in the United States began to seek means of rescuing their European comrades.

In November 1933, an organization called the Jewish Labor Committee was organized by well-known socialist, B. Vladek.[2] Vladek was a great humanitarian, not narrow or sectarian. His aim in organizing the Jewish Labor Committee was to rescue and assist those had fled from Nazi terror, and I believe that if he had been alive at the time of the Nazi invasion of the rest of Europe, many of our comrades would not have perished at the hands of Hitler's executioners.

With the help of the AFL and of some of the larger unions the Jewish Labor Committee managed to obtain a considerable number of visas to allow entry into the United States for people in Europe whose lives were in danger. At that time the internationally known Anarchist, Alexander Schapiro, was in Marseilles, where he was in charge of rescue work for the Jewish Emigrant Society. In 1940 he sent a telegram to our comrades in New York, advising them to compile a list of our comrades in France and to present it to the Jewish Labor Committee with a request that the names should be included on their list so that the rescue of our comrades might be hastened.

A list was accordingly prepared in New York, sent to us in Chicago for the addition of any names we knew, and then presented by a local delegation to the Jewish Labor Committee, whose members gave an assurance that they would take care of the matter. A few weeks later our friends in New York asked the JLC what was being done for our comrades in Europe, and they were told that our list had got lost somewhere in the office. A new list was presented, which the JLC promised very solemnly to treat with great care, and once more we settled down to await the results.

Meanwhile the situation in Europe became worse every day, and our Jewish comrades in Paris were being forced to flee or to go into hiding so as not to be caught and sent away to German concentration camps. The following letter, from a friend who later escaped, gives a full picture of the kind of life which Jewish radicals in France were undergoing at the time:

October 7, 1940

My dear ones,

Your letters were most welcome. You advise us against going home. Well now, even if we would want to return, it's too late. "Foreigners, Jewish and colored people must not enter the occupied zone." This is the decision of our new master.

Our friends with whom we lived in the village had to give up their house and to go to the south of France. Hence, we went down to Clermont—the town nearby. We had no idea that even in the same state the foreigner hasn't the right to move about. So, we went down with the intention to find here some work. Imagine our state of mind when we were told we had no right to come here, no right to work, and that we must "stay where we were!" After

48 hours we were mighty glad to be registered—even if we had to promise that we wouldn't try to look for a job.

Here we occupy a small room with friends of friends—good Catholics. Without any members of our family near us, and without work, our life is very dreary. The weather too is cold and nasty, and we have only a few summer things with us. Last week I wrote to my sisters and brothers and asked if they couldn't send us some of their worn clothes, which would keep us warm. But I have an idea that there is something wrong with my people. I didn't hear from them since the beginning of May! Enclosed herewith you will find their address. Would you kindly drop them a line and give them my new address? Maybe my letters didn't reach them, and they keep on writing to Paris.

A few days ago, we had a letter from Rose in which she tells us to get out as quickly as possible, never mind where. I suppose this is a decision, which you all took. But, my dearest ones, this is absolutely impossible. If we have no visas we cannot move. I asked Alexander, who is in the immigration office, to tell me what we could do in order to get out as quickly as possible, and he told us not to budge from here, but to cable to Rose that she should compel Dubinsky to put us on the political refugee list for visitor's visas. He, I mean Senya, is very much surprised that Dubinsky could not be induced to accept the list of names which Mratchny presented to him. He advises haste, because after the 31st of October the visitors' visas will not be given any more.

But a cable means 200 francs, so I decided to send two letters by airmail instead. For I know that you, my loved ones, are doing all in your power anyway. Alexander is very nice, and he wants to help us, but—as he says—without a visa he can do nothing.

Please write to us; we can get all the mail you send. It is the only bright spot now—a letter from a friend.

Mollie[3]

While letters like this came to us, one after another, we waited anxiously, hoping every day for news from the Jewish Labor Committee, but the weeks ran away without our hearing anything, until our patience was exhausted, and a delegation again went to the Jewish Labor Committee to ask about the fate of our comrades abroad. We were astonished to be told that the list had again been "lost." After this it became clear to us that history was repeating itself; in the old Tsarist prisons the Social Democrats, in charge of funds from abroad collected for all political prisoners, had refused to help our comrades, and now, half a century later, their descendants were again showing their hatred of the libertarians.

In Russia before 1917 the actions of the Social Democrats had not resulted in loss of life, but now it was a different matter, and it is impossible to find any excuse for the inhuman attitude of the Socialists in this situation. The people of the Jewish Labor Committee made great capital of the six million Jews killed in Germany or by German armies, but when it was actually possible for them to save a small group of Jewish people, and a few others who were not Jewish, they left these people to the mercy of the Nazis, merely because of the difference in political faith.

This attitude on the part of the Social Democrats naturally evoked strong protest, and it was suggested that we should expose the attitude of the JLC in the *Freie Arbeiter Stimme*, but our Jewish comrades in New York opposed this because they still hoped that something might be done to save some of our people, but as far as the JLC was concerned, their hopes were in vain.

But before I leave this question, I should like to say that if the Jewish Labor Committee had refused in the beginning to do anything to help us save a few of our comrades, nobody would have thought a great deal about it, since from past experience we knew their attitude towards our movement. What I condemn is that for political reasons they made a promise they had no intention of keeping. If only they had declared openly that they wished to help only Socialists, instead of pretending to be a nonpartisan organization, we should never have gone to them in the first place.

Later on, in 1942, our people made another attempt through the Jewish Labor Committee to get some Mexican visas for comrades who wished to escape from Europe, and I wrote to ask Alexander Schapiro whether he thought anything would come of this. He replied: "When the new list for Mexico was made up, the names of our people were last. Tania (his wife) then went to the Committee (the JLC) and, thanks to our connections, and especially because I was directing the emigration work in Paris, Marseilles, and later, Lisbon, and was in this way connected with the JLC, our list of names will definitely be included in the new list."

He spoke with undue optimism, as can be seen from this letter from two comrades who had the good luck to escape from Europe and who tell here the grim story of persecution in Europe and of indifference in the JLC:

Mexico, Nov. 1st, 1942

Dear Comrade Yelensky:

I have written you long ago, but never received an answer. However, I just found out that you have done what you could to be of help to our unfortunate family in France.

Enclosed herewith is a letter from Volin in which he acknowledges the receipt of 25 dollars, which came from Chicago. I understand that you sent the money. That is why I am sending this acknowledgment to you—in case no other has reached you now—this letter may be of use to you.

You will be glad to know that in May of this year we sent 40 dollars. In June, New York sent 100 dollars, and now, as there came a desperate call for help saying that what was sent was not enough, we mailed 55 dollars from here to New York, and Alexander immediately added 95 and sent it off to Marseilles for distribution.

The last news we have from France is extremely sad. The persecution grows beyond all description or imagination! The Spaniards who recently came told us that the persecution of the Jewish people in France is something unbelievable! The only consoling thing is that there is at the same time a spirit of solidarity on the part of the French, which is making up a good deal for the cruelty, humiliation, and savagery to which the Jewish people are subjected. We ourselves have proof of this.

When Eva S. (a very good friend) was arrested and sent to Gurs (Basses Pyrenees) Jeanne W., a French woman, who is only a friend of ours, went down to the camp, was there for two days, and tried every possible way to get her out. Alas, she did not succeed, but the fact that she went down there is a big sacrifice—for she put her own liberty at danger.

We are trying hard to obtain visas (of which I have already spoken to you once) for Eva S., Jacques D., and Nicholas T. When Rose was here in April, I gave her the list which she gave to J. Patt when in NY. Imagine that when Alexander called J. Patt and asked what about them, the reply was that those named do not exist on the list!!! In another words, they were just ignored! Now, A.S. was assured that they will be attended to. But I will not believe those people until we see results.

Do write us a few lines. I think that we can help our folks much more if we would be more united, keep in close touch with each other, and inform one another of our doings.

From S. and M.

To conclude this account of our efforts to get Anarchist refugees out of Europe through the Jewish Labor Committee, as far as I know only two of our comrades were saved from the Germans in France through the actions of the JLC, and if they had not had many powerful friends in the International Garment Workers' Union, they would have experienced the same fate as so many other libertarians in France.

IX

POSTWAR ACTIVITIES, 1945

During and after the Second World War the Alexander Berkman Fund was not concerned only with the largely unsuccessful attempt to get Anarchists out of Europe. It was also concerned with the problem of providing help for those who remained and, after the war was over, for those who had survived. The few hundred dollars, which was in the treasury at the outbreak of the war, did not last long; indeed, it was a mere pittance in comparison with the amount that would have been needed to do anything effective. Moreover, our appeals brought in very little; this was due partly to the fact that many of our people were scared by the political situation produced by the war, but also to the great publicity which other organizations used to create the impression that they were looking after everybody who needed help. Here and there our friends collected a few dollars, but it was not done in a systematic way, and it did not go very far.

We soon realized that both lack of funds and the impossibility of reaching our comrades in the occupied countries made it difficult for us to do anything to help them during the actual war years. But we also knew that the slaughter in Europe would not last forever, and that those comrades who escaped with their lives would have to be helped as soon as the war reached its end. We were well aware that this great task could not be fulfilled by Chicago alone and, having discussed the matter, we decided to send one of our members to the eastern states in order to establish personal contact with groups and individuals.

I undertook to make this trip, and in three weeks I visited Washington, Philadelphia, New York, Stelton (New Jersey), Mohegan (New York), Cleveland, and Detroit. Everywhere I held meetings in which I brought out the tragic facts about the failure to rescue our comrades from Europe, exposed the inadequacies of the Jewish Labor Committee, and appealed to my audiences to prepare for the work that would have to be started as soon as the war came to an end. These personal contacts brought good results in the ensuing years, and as soon as the call for help came from Europe there were friends in many cities who became extremely active in helping our comrades in need.

When Paris was liberated from the Germans, the Alexander Berkman Aid Fund immediately sent out letters to every address in that city which was in our files. As soon as the replies began to trickle in, we sent money, and slowly, in return, there came news regarding the fate of our friends. In February 1945, for instance, we received a note from Sam Frydman's brother, who was in the American army. He wrote: "Yesterday I saw Michelle (Sam Frydman's daughter). She is skinny and sickly-looking. The $25, which you sent, she received. We hope that Sam and Dora will return alive from the German concentration camps."

Alas, as I have already said, Sam and Dora were among those we did not return. A month later, in March 1945, Alexander Schapiro wrote to us from New York: "I have just had a letter from Paris, from Kantorovich. He tells me that the following were deported (presumably to Germany): David Poliakoff, Michel Finkelstein, Morris Schantz (his wife Fania remained in Paris), Fruchtman and his wife, Buzi Frishberg, Sarah Elstein and her daughter, Israel Beck, Schmulek Matsidlover, Victor Bruth, Goldberg, and many others whose names he will give us in a future letter. Among those who have been saved we have, in Paris, Teitelbaum and Anna Schwartsbard, besides Yania and Eva Schwartz in Lyons. Viola is in Marseille."

Afterwards more and more tragic news came in from all over Europe of comrades who had been killed or had vanished without a clue to their fate.

To cope with the calls for help, the Alexander Berkman Fund sent out a countrywide appeal for help, and this time over $5,000 came in; this enabled us to broaden our activities and to send help to France, Italy, Germany, Austria, England, Poland, and North Africa. In addition to our own activities, groups in many centers were participating in the urgent task of relief. The Jewish Federation in New York decided at its annual conference to reorganize its International Aid Fund into a Libertarian Refugee Fund, and its affiliated Los Angeles and Detroit groups organized similar funds. The Mohegan group set up a special relief committee. The English-speaking magazine *Why* in New York, and the Italian groups centered round *L'Adunata*, collected funds for refugees, the SIA concentrated its help on the thousands of Spanish refugees in France and North Africa, a committee in Mexico City set to work collecting funds for Europe, and later on groups in London, England, become active in the relief work.

Yet, despite all this activity, it became clear to us, that we could not help in a completely satisfactory way all those who had suffered so much and were still suffering. All our relief and help organizations operated virtually without overhead expense, since all administrative work was done as a free contribution towards our cause, but now, with so many to help, we had to be more careful than ever in counting every penny we spent; every committee, in fact, worked splendidly at getting the most out of the funds at its command.

One problem that concerned us was that of making fair distribution of our funds at such a distance, and when Yania Doubinsky came to back to Paris from Lyons in 1945 the Alexander Berkman Aid Fund suggested to him that he should form a Paris section of the Fund and set up a systematic distribution of the help we were sending to France, in such a way that the most needy comrades would always be helped first. We also suggested that this work should be done in connection with the SIA in Paris. Doubinsky accepted our suggestion and organized a committee, which worked under the title of the Paris Section of the Alexander Berkman Aid Fund. In 1946, after this arrangement had been in operation for some time, both the Paris Section and the SIA in Paris sent reports for inclusion in a 24-page pamphlet which we published to celebrate the 25th anniversary of the Alexander Berkman Fund;[1] I am now reprinting these reports for the insight they give into the actual work that was going on among needy European libertarians at this time:

> 1. Activity Report, Alexander Berkman Aid Fund, Paris Section.
> Many packages of food and clothing have been shipped to France on the request of the Paris Section of the Alexander Berkman Aid Fund. This help was sent by the A. Berkman Aid Fund (Chicago

Section), and the Libertarian Refugee Fund which was organized by the Jewish Anarchist Federation of the United States and is composed of the New York, Los Angeles and Detroit groups, as well as Mexican and English comrades.

Most of the parcels were sent directly to the needy comrades of the Masseube camp, to comrades in sanitariums and hospitals, and to individual comrades in need. Besides these parcels, 231 packages were received directly by the Paris Section of the A. Berkman Aid Fund, and they were distributed in conjunction with the Paris SIA among the more needy of our comrades.

Our committee was organized through the initiative of the A. Berkman Aid Fund in Chicago, and it is made up of the most responsible comrades who were willing to do the work. Immediately they started the distribution of the aid that came from Chicago.

Soon thereafter lists of needy comrades were compiled and were forwarded to Chicago. These names were added to the lists, which the Chicago comrades already had. When other American comrades in New York, Detroit, and especially Los Angeles came to our aid we were able to help many more needy comrades.

Jewish comrades who were able to escape and survive Hitler's inferno, Spanish and other comrades, who returned from concentration camps, hospitals, and sanitariums, were able to receive our help. Through the SIA in Paris we obtained the address of many unfortunate comrades, many of them invalids as a result of their participation in the Spanish Revolution, and food and clothing were forthcoming as a result of our efforts.

Notwithstanding the continuous aid from our American comrades, aid is still greatly needed. Reaction still reigns in Spain and many of our comrades cross the border to France, paying no heed to the danger of crossing the border without proper identification. Almost daily, young people, proud and courageous, come to France. They are penniless. They need food, shelter, and clothing. We believe our efforts to help them must be continued.

2. Letters from the International Anti-Fascist Solidarity (SIA), Paris, November 13, 1946.

We are sending you an itemized list, which describes the type of help you have been giving the Spanish refugees and which was distributed to them through the SIA. The SIA, as you well know, is made up of Anarchists and Spanish Libertarians exiled in France.

Fifty percent of the Spanish refugees in France belong to the SIA. Notwithstanding the fact that the organization is responsible for the care of 70 percent of its members, the SIA does not receive any government or semi-official aid. The reason for this lack of help is because the organization is the spiritual child of our beloved CNT-FAI and hence its orientation is antigovernment.

The aid for the Spanish refugees, which comes from foreign countries, is distributed by the pseudo-Republican government and the distribution is made not according to need but rather in accordance with the political influence of the refugees. This explains why your help, though very valuable, is far from sufficient in answering the needs of our refugee comrades.

It must also be remembered that our comrades were compelled to move many times since the Spanish events, which has resulted in the loss of much of their personal belongings; that the majority of us have lived in exile for almost ten years and in comparison with other workers, have been often forced to work under disadvantageous conditions; and also, that we do not expect any government help whatsoever even in the most dire cases, such as for invalids, the wounded, and old age.

Your brotherly hand has helped us materially, but more than materially it has aided us spiritually for it has displayed that international solidarity still lives.

In addition to our activities in France, we tried to organize a German section, but this proved impossible, largely owing to the divisions between the various military zones. We did however succeed in persuading comrades in the various large cities to form local committees, which distributed necessities and money according to need and reduced to a minimum the possibility of unfair distribution.

During the period immediately after the war, when help was most urgently needed in Europe, money alone was often of little use owing to the difficulty of buying food and clothing in the countries involved. In consequence of this situation, requests for direct gifts and clothing began to reach us, and we had to branch out in a new direction.

Fortunately, CARE began to function at this time, and the relief funds in both Chicago and New York sent thousands of packages through this organization, while thousands more were packed and sent off by the members of the various relief committees. Apart from food and clothing, we sent dress materials, thread, medicines—anything that might be needed to keep human existence going, and we dispatched such quantities of used clothing and bedding that all our comrades in urgent need of such items were supplied. All the groups I have named earlier took part in this task of sending parcels directly to Europe, but many also contributed cash to the Alexander Berkman Aid Fund or the Libertarian Refugee Fund in New York. The Los Angeles Libertarian Relief Fund particularly distinguished itself by the large number of parcels which it sent.

Before ending this description of our activities during the years immediately after the war, I would like to reproduce a letter we received from the Spanish refugees in the camp at Masseube, France; it gives some idea of the kind of problems to which we were trying to find a solution.

> Masseube, France, Nov. 12, 1946
>
> I received your letter written on October 28, 1946, in which you inform us that the Alexander Berkman Committee sent us four big CARE packages. So far, we have received none of them, but we have already written to the CARE office in Paris, inquiring about them. We are very glad to hear from you that you ordered us ten more packages; as soon as we receive them we will let you know.
>
> About two months ago all the very sick comrades and the elderly ones who lived in this camp were taken to the hospitals and rest places of this province.

There they are getting the necessary care, with the exception of food, which is lacking in France. At the same time, I want to tell you that all these comrades, although they are in different hospitals, are receiving their share of whatever you send. We have a responsible committee that distributes everything equally.

As regards stockings, there are only three women who belong to our Local Federation. However, there are women, the wives and daughters of our comrades, who are not members of the organization, but who will help us fight for the cause, and the stockings will be well received by them. I also want to tell you that in the packages you sent us previously, there were women's clothes and stockings. We gave a small share to each wife and child of our comrades and sent the rest to the Department Committee of the SIA in Gers in order to distribute them among the more needy. We did that only with women's and children's clothing, and not with men's wear, because we did not have enough of that for those who needed it. There are several comrades who do not have overcoats and shoes.

E. Fernández Negrete
Delegate of the Local Federation of
The Spanish Libertarian Movement

There is a story attached to the stockings mentioned in this letter. In Chicago we had a comrade named Joe Goldman. We were then searching for clothing or anything else of this kind that we could obtain, and as Joe had a sister-in-law who held a high position in a firm of sportswear manufacturers, I asked him if he thought he could get anything through her. He promised to try.

A week or two later Goldman rang me up and asked me to find a truck and take away from his workshop the goods his sister had sent him. I thought Goldman was joking, but when I came to him a few days later and he took me into his stockroom, I saw that it was no joke at all. There were five very large packages, and when we opened them, we found over a hundred dozen pairs of stockings, as well as many jumpers, and other important things, such as woolen swimming suits from which we could made under-shirts. Thus, though we could not supply our comrades with everything they needed, there were stockings enough for everybody.

As economic conditions improved in Europe, and our own income from funds grew smaller, a certain amount of reconstruction of our activities became necessary. Many of the smaller groups and committees, which had been active in sending relief to Europe immediately after the war, ceased their work, and after 1950 only the organizations in Chicago, New York, and Los Angeles remained active. The last two decided to concentrate their activities on the work, which had in the past been done by the International Aid Fund and to help old and sick comrades. The Alexander Berkman Aid Fund returned to the work of helping polit-ical prisoners and internees.

Its immediate concern became to help members of the Bulgarian movement, both those in Bulgaria itself and also those who had escaped from that country through Yugoslavia and Greece, most of whom were held in Greek concentration camps. During the past five years our work has been concentrated on the assistance of political pris-oners in Italy, Bulgaria, and, particularly, in Spain, where there are thousands of imprisoned Anarchists whose families are in urgent need of help. In this connection the Spanish movement collects large sums of money, and what help we can give is only a drop in the ocean in comparison.

X

CONSERVATISM AND FACTIONALISM

The first postwar years brought in considerable sums of money, particularly through the yearly appeals sent out by the Alexander Berkman Aid Fund and affiliated groups of the Jewish Federation. But by the third and fourth years after the end of hostilities we began to notice that the financial response to our appeals was becoming progressively smaller. It is true that in some directions our needs had decreased. The German comrades, for instance, found that they were becoming more secure materially and decided to accept no further help from us. Some of the Spaniards in the French camps were placed in public institutions, and they too declined any more assistance. But we still had on our hands a large number of people who needed help urgently, and for them, with our reduced income, we could not provide even the minimum amount we had sent before.

In this situation we were forced to think of means by which we could find additional funds, and at one of our meetings it was suggested that we should once again approach the Jewish Labor Committee in New York.[1] Because of our past experience, many of us were opposed to this, but the majority thought there was nothing to be lost by making another effort. I was delegated to go to New York, and,

in preparation for my trip, a committee of the Alexander
Berkman Aid Fund called upon the chairman of the Chicago
Jewish Labor Committee, J. [Julius] Siegel. When he heard
our case, Seigel agreed that I should go to New York, and he
wrote a letter of recommendation to N. [Nathan] Chanin,
the chairman of the JLC Office Committee.

In February 1947, I arrived in New York and almost
immediately went to see Chanin, presenting Siegel's letter
of recommendation and stating our case. When I finished,
Chanin replied: "I don't see any reason why your organization shouldn't receive help from us." He had added
that the best thing would be for a delegation representing the Alexander Berkman Aid Fund to meet the Office
Committee of the JLC. When I heard this, I thought a
miracle had happened, but I was soon to find how wrong
my impression was.

After seeing Chanin I went to a meeting of the Jewish
Federation in New York and told them what happened. They
decided to send a delegation, as Chanin had suggested, but,
since I could stay no longer in New York, I was unable to be
a member of it. A few weeks later, however, news reached
Chicago from the Jewish Federation that the delegation had
presented our case to the Office Committee of the Jewish
Labor Committee, which had granted a sum of $2,500 for
a group of our comrades in Poland to establish a printing
shop. As regards the general question about funds for refugees, they promised to give early consideration to this matter.

We waited five months without receiving any news as
to what the Jewish Labor Committee had decided to do
for our refugees, and in the end the Alexander Berkman
Aid Fund asked its chairman, Irving S. Abrams, to write to
the JLC on the matter. He wrote to N. Chanin as follows
on July 5th, 1947:

Dear Friend Chanin:

I am writing you at this time to bring to your attention a matter, which has been a source of irritation for some time and is making our situation very difficult.

Last February we delegated our secretary, Comrade Boris Yelensky, to go to New York and solicit the Jewish Labor Committee to grant us assistance on behalf of our comrades in Europe, whose requests for assistance have been increasing steadily.

Before Comrade Yelensky left for New York, we discussed the matter with Friend J. Siegel, and he advised us to take the matter up with you and gave Comrade Yelensky a letter of introduction to you. Comrade Yelensky reported to us that he discussed the matter with you, and you suggested that a committee of our New York comrades appear before the Office Committee. We referred the matter to the Jewish Anarchist Federation and have been informed that a committee appeared before the Office Committee of the Jewish Labor Committee and requested assistance in our work in Poland and other European countries.

The Committee reports to us that the Office Committee advised them that the Jewish Labor Committee has made an allotment for Poland and would consider our request for other work. To date we have not received any word from the office of the Jewish Labor Committee.

A number of years ago we complained that our comrades were being slighted and engaged in considerable correspondence with New York.

Nevertheless, we have continued in our assistance and support of the Jewish Labor Committee.

We know that our comrades in Los Angeles, Detroit, New York and other cities have contributed liberally to work and money and the fact that I am chairman of the Workmen's Circle Division this year indicates clearly our desire to cooperate and help in this work. However, if we did not assist in the work, our comrades in Europe would still be entitled to assistance, and I have been requested to write to you and ascertain if the Jewish Labor Committee intends to help us in our work. I am awaiting your reply.

Fraternally Yours,

(signed) Irving S. Abrams

On July 14th, 1947, we received an answer from the Jewish Labor Committee. It did not come from Chanin himself, and, though we can only make conjectures about his reason for passing the task to someone else, it seems possible that he did not wish to offend Abrams, who had been very active in the work of the Jewish Labor Committee in Chicago, by a direct rebuff. The letter was actually signed by B. [Benjamin] Tabachinsky, and I reproduce it below.

Jewish Labor Committee

175 E. Broadway

New York, New York

July 13, 1947

Friend Irving Abrams

Alexander Berkman Relief Fund

Chicago, Illinois

Dear Friend Abrams:

I write you a reply, in replace [*sic*] of Chanin,

concerning the matter about which you inquire in your letter. I want to say in that connection that your people, who informed you about the matter as to how we conduct our relief work for your friends in Europe, have truly not given the correct information.

Let us try to clarify the matter for you with the facts. The group of your people in France totals—according to my knowledge since I was there—at the maximum, 25–30 persons. In the course of the year, we sent them in cash $3,000.00, which we have done for no other group—not even a third of that. We provided the funds in this manner: For the Cooperative, $2,000.00, and later an additional $1,000, just as we had promised your friends in California.

We have also reached an understanding with the Manager of Local 117 to provide them with five sewing machines. The machines are already here. We need only the possibility of transporting them, and that is not within our power. It is a fact, however, that the machines are already at their disposal. If it were within our power to bring the same help to the other groups, we would be happy to do so. We provided the five machines for your friends because I have made such a promise. To be sure, I thought at that time that we would be able to gather a larger number of sewing machines, but we are keeping our promise.

With regards to packages and other forms of assistance, that is being taken care of in the same degree as to our other friends.

For the foregoing you will be able to see that the information, which you have received, is not correct.

I am pleased that I can rectify the matter by presenting the facts.

With cordial regards,
B. TABACHINSKY
Executive Secretary

The true facts are that I did not go to see Chanin in New York in order to talk to him about the cooperative workshop in Paris. What we asked, and what Tabachinsky significantly ignores in his letter, was help for the thousands of hungry, ill-clothed, and sick individuals who were on our lists of refugees.

Furthermore, the Alexander Berkman Committee had nothing to do with the cooperative. What I talked to Chanin about, and what the New York Committee of the Jewish Federation asked for, was help for all our comrades in Europe.

The final point to be emphasized in connection with Tabachinsky's letter is that he tries to impress upon Abrams the smallness of our movement by saying, "the group of your people in France totals—according to my knowledge, since I was there—at a maximum, 25–30 persons." In this way he seeks to create the impression of generosity on the part of the Jewish Labor Committee for having given so much to so few people.

In fact, in Paris alone the people under our care amounted, not 25–30, but to several hundreds. And even if we leave aside this deliberate misrepresentation of facts, other small groups received, in proportion, far more than the Anarchists in France. During the period when relief was being organized, the Jewish Labor Committee collected millions of dollars, of which a considerable proportion came from groups containing strong libertarian elements.

Out of this great sum the Anarchists in Europe received the following help; the figures are taken from a list, which Tabachinsky sent to Abrams with his letter:

To 3 persons to come to Mexico and USA	$ 1,050
To Frydman's child	5,000 fr.
For a French paper in Paris	$ 500
For the cooperative in Paris	$ 3,000
For a printing shop in Poland	$ 2,500
Total	$ 7,050 and 5,000 francs.

During this period the JLC also sent about 40 food parcels to our people and paid a small amount (unspecified) for clothing to the Paris JLC.

It will be seen that there is in fact no provision indicated in Tabachinsky's figures for Anarchist refugees in general, and in reality, all that the Jewish Labor Committee ever did for our comrades was to help a few isolated individuals when a particular pressure happened to be brought to bear upon them. As Alexander Shapiro suggested, what this so-called nonpartisan organization gave to the libertarians was "in the form of a bribe" to avoid public protest.

Our experience with the Jewish Labor Committee showed that we could get very little positive help from organizations dominated by Socialists. Even worse was the fact that Socialist influences worked against us in connection with various nonpolitical organizations which at one time or another gave their support to the work of the Alexander Berkman Aid Fund. To give one example, the large Jewish fraternal organization known as the Workmen's Circle for many years endorsed at its conventions our work in helping political prisoners in Russia and gave an annual donation to our funds. In 1939, as usual we sent an appeal telegram to the Workmen's

Circle Convention, but that year we received no donation. We accordingly sent a note of inquiry, and received this answer:

> Dear Friend Yelensky:
> Our donation of $300 for the Russian Prisoners was sent to Mrs. Strunsky, the Treasurer of this Fund for the past two years.
>
> Sincerely yours,
J. BASKIN, General Secretary
Workmen's Circle

Mrs. Strunsky, it should be explained, was the head of the committee, which helped the Socialists in Russian prisons; in this way the Anarchists were squeezed entirely out of the help given by the Workmen's Circle conventions.

In 1944, for the sake of the record, the Alexander Berkman Aid Fund made a further attempt to gain endorsement of our work from the Workmen's Circle, and also a donation, as in the past. This time we received the following letter:

> The Workmen's Circle
175 East Broadway
New York, N.Y.
January 10, 1944
>
> Alexander Berkman Aid Fund Committee
> 2422 North Halsted Street
> Chicago, Illinois
> Dear Friends:
> We are in receipt of your letter asking for an endorsement of your committee to the branches of the Workmen's Circle and also for a direct contribution for purposes indicating in your letter.

We wish to inform you that since the Workmen's Circle is an integral part of the Jewish Labor Committee and all our work for the aid of refugees is done through that committee, we have therefore referred your request to them for consideration.

Fraternally yours,
National Executive Committee
Workmen's Circle
J. BASKIN, General Secretary

Once again, we had been passed over in favor of a Socialist-dominated organization—and that by the Workmen's Circle, of whose rank-and-file membership at least 95 percent had no connection with social-democratic political parties.

Later on we had a similar experience with the International Ladies' Garment Workers' Union. Originally the union was friendly, as can be seen from the following extract from the Proceedings of the 26th Convention of the Union in Cleveland, Ohio, in 1947:

Delegate Jacob Katz appeared before your committee to ask for financial assistance to the Alexander Berkman Fund, an organization that is rendering assistance to individuals needy of the labor movement all over the world.

The record of our International indicates that this fund is listed among the many organizations who have heretofore received financial assistance. Your committee, therefore, refers this matter to the incoming GEB for continued support.

The same decision applies to the request by the same delegate for assistance to the International Aid

Fund, an associate organization of the Alexander Berkman Aid Fund.

(Upon motion this portion of the report was adopted.)

Until the Chicago convention of the union in 1953 we received donations from the ILGWU funds. At the convention the financial assistance ceased, and, though we wrote several times to David Dubinsky, the president of the union, he did not see fit to reply to our letter. In the days of a bitter strike when the ILGWU was organized many members of our Jewish movement took an active part in its formation, and to this day there are a few old anarchists among its vice-presidents and its top-level executives. But now, when it comes to helping Anarchists outside its ranks, the union chooses to ignore our appeals.

If space allowed, I could bring out many more facts which would bear upon this matter of the exclusion of our activities from aid they had formerly gained from the organized labor movement, but I think what I have quoted is sufficient to show how people who formerly used our movement and its members are now glad to ignore it. The unfortunate thing is that so many people, for one reason or another, still give their help to organizations which are hostile to libertarian ideals.

We were grateful for the help, but we still felt that Anarchists were not receiving their full share of the millions of relief money that had been collected, much of it with libertarian help. Perhaps this is a promise of the day when solidarity among radicals will be revived, and it will no longer be necessary to have their own relief program; it is evident to us that this day has not yet arrived.

Actually, we are passing through a conservative period, which has made it difficult for all radicals. The general decline of our funds cannot have been due to lack of financial means, nor do we think that our efforts have been weaker, or the need less.

While we hope for a return to more favorable conditions, the time may have come for a rethinking of the needs and opportunities of the workers, and of our mission and tactics. May the decline of the program of the past make way for a new and united radicalism of greater vision, freedom, and strength.

TWENTY-FIFTH JUBILEE ANNIVERSARY OF THE ALEXANDER BERKMAN AID FUND

By B. [Benjamin] Axler, Secretary,
Jewish Anarchist Federation

Our comrades in Chicago, who devoted themselves particularly to relief work on behalf of political prisoners and needy comrades—under the name of "Berkman Hilfs-Fund" (Berkman Aid Fund), are presently celebrating the 25th jubilee anniversary of the Fund. The details of their activities are set forth in two articles by Chaver B. Yelensky, which have been published in the *Freie Arbeiter Stimme*.

Following World War II, the comrades of the Chicago Berkman Fund plunged into this relief work for the sake of our surviving comrades in various countries.

The need was so great, and the relief efforts so urgent, that our Federation likewise found it necessary to reorganize the "Interaid Fund" and to set up a Libertarian Refugee Fund, and to conduct assistance on a larger scale—a project which we continue to this very day. For a time, the Chicago comrades of the Berkman Fund regarded the Libertarian Refugee Fund as a competitive undertaking, or at best as an overlapping, duplicating effort. Later on, however, they realized that the need was so great, and help was so desperately needed that there was room for two relief organizations, in addition to the sections of the Los Angeles and Detroit. The New York and Chicago relief groups soon came to a harmonious understanding, allocated regions for their relief work and now cooperate in their endeavors, even though they operate autonomously. Let us hope that we may soon see the day when it may be possible to liquidate both these Funds.

Now, upon arriving at the 25th jubilee anniversary of the Berkman Fund and upon concluding a year's activity, the Chicago comrades have issued a 24-page brochure, containing a biography of Alexander Berkman; an historical survey of the Berkman Fund; also letters of appreciation from needy comrades who have been assisted, and a financial report—all in English. The brochure has been distributed to all comrades and readers of the *Freie Arbeiter Stimme*, so as to acquaint them with, and report to them on, this activity.

Hence, we for our part wish at this time to direct the attention of the *Freie Arbeiter Stimme* readers, and of our comrades in particular, to the importance of this undertaking through all these years and especially the past two years, on the part of the Chicago division of the Berkman Fund. The Chicago Berkman Fund, under the leadership of B. Yelensky, carries on a large-scale and ramified relief effort, and our comrades ought to cooperate with them eagerly and generously.

We, the comrades of our Federation, esteem highly the endeavors of the Chicago comrades and encourage them to continue their efforts to extend aid to the imprisoned, persecuted and impoverished comrades wherever they may be found. It is only our wish that there should be no necessity for celebrating any more jubilees of relief funds; that we should be able to devote our energy and activity towards the enlightenment of the masses and the propagation of the anarchist ideal in its struggle for a better and freer society.

THE LATVIAN ANARCHIST RED CROSS AND THE LEXINGTON AVENUE EXPLOSION

by Matt Hart

For over 120 years, the Anarchist Black Cross (known in its earliest years as the Anarchist Red Cross) has dedicated itself to the liberation of political prisoners. The organization's activities have spread to every corner of the earth. But despite its long history, much of the organization's past remains relatively hidden from view. Although Boris Yelensky's book, *The Struggle for Equality,* has done much to uncover a significant portion of the organization's past, the book does omit certain moments, either intentionally or unintentionally. Through his omission, Yelensky excludes one of the most significant incidents involving the organization in North America. In July 1914, the Latvian section of the Anarchist Red Cross engaged in a plot to assassinate John D. Rockefeller for his hand in the Ludlow Massacre. The plan was designed to strike back against the brutality of capitalism; however, the plan failed when the bomb designated for Rockefeller prematurely exploded. The explosion left three stories of a Lexington Avenue tenement destroyed and four individuals dead. While the event (known as the Lexington Avenue explosion) has been recorded in the annals of the anarchist movement, it has not found its rightful place in history of the Anarchist Black Cross.

THE EARLY YEARS

The early Anarchist Red Cross (ARC) was born out of the revolutionary struggle in Russia. As revolutionaries faced persecution at the hands of the Tsarist regime, the anarchist movement needed to form an organization to guarantee that aid was given to anarchists imprisoned for revolutionary activities. Exiled communities in Europe and North America formed chapters to ensure international support continued for those held in Russian prisons. Many of those involved in prisoner support had been previously imprisoned or exiled for their involvement in the 1905 Revolution. After they escaped, or were released, they continued their activity outside the Russian borders, predominately in France, England, and the United States. The ARC provided support for the unfortunate ones who were left behind.

The purpose of the ARC was primarily to support anarchists imprisoned in Russia. But, by 1913, other groups emerged to focus on anarchists imprisoned in other regions of Eastern Europe and the Russian Empire. One such organization was the Latvian section of the Anarchist Red Cross, which focused on imprisoned anarchists in Latvia. Three individuals associated with the Latvian ARC were Carl Hanson, Charles Berg, and Louise Berger.[1]

Both Berg and Hanson were born in Latvia. Berg, known by his friends as the "Big Swede," was born in 1891 in the city of Angern [now Engure] in the region of Courland. However, according to an interview in the *New York Times* by a man claiming to be Berg's brother, the name "Berg" was an alias; his real name was Peter Fischer.[2] Latvian revolutionaries of the period often used aliases as an elementary security precaution. Most were involved in the 1905 Revolution in the Baltic region, and an uncertain fate awaited them should they be sent back. Berg was no exception.

His father was a wealthy shipowner and was able to give his son a good education. While he was in school, a strike broke out among the students, and Charles, one of the most active militants, was expelled. In the 1905 Revolution, at the age of fourteen, he assisted through the distribution of revolutionary propaganda, using religious services to spread this "new religion." Later that year, he became a member of a guerilla group active in the Baltic region known as the Forest Brethren. After the group broke up, he continued his revolutionary involvement through transporting arms across the Russian border. For several years, he worked as a merchant seaman, as did Carl Hanson.[3]

Hanson's childhood was very similar to that of Berg. By the age of nine, he was already involved in organizing fellow students against the teacher's lesson plans. By fifteen he began working at a machine shop and was fired six months later for his involvement in a strike. His next job at a silk mill met the same fate. The two men met working as merchant sailors in Hamburg, Germany. After working together and becoming close friends, they headed to New York in 1911, where they found work as carpenters.[4] Hanson was later fired from his job on a Long Island bridge for distributing anarchist literature to fellow workers.

Hanson's decision to come to America was influenced in large part by his half-sister, Louise Berger, also a revolutionary anarchist. According to the *New York Times*, Berger was an orphan in Germany. She traveled to the United States around 1908. Soon after their arrival, the three anarchists joined the Latvian Anarchist Group, a group involved in the publication of anarchist literature. When a few comrades organized a Latvian Anarchist Red Cross in December 1913, the three joined to assist the imprisoned anarchists in their homeland.[5]

During this time, Berg, Berger, and Hanson also joined the ranks of the Anti-Military League and became active in the movement for the unemployed. Berg was the assistant treasurer of the Conference of the Unemployed at the Ferrer Center. The Ferrer Center was part of the Modern School movement and was the hub for organizing around the free speech and unemployment movements taking place in the region. Alexander Berkman, Emma Goldman, Luigi Galleani, as well as many individuals from the Anarchist Red Cross, spent a great deal of their time at the Ferrer Center.[6]

FROM LUDLOW TO LEXINGTON AVENUE

On April 20, 1914, one of the worst atrocities against the US labor movement took place in Ludlow, Colorado, when National Guardsmen opened fire on a tent colony of striking mine workers and their families. A pitched battle ensued throughout the day between the guardsmen and the striking miners. As the miners retreated into the countryside, guardsmen entered the tent colony to soak the tents with kerosene and set them on fire. In one of the tents eleven children and two women were hiding from the strafing bullets in a cellar dug underneath the tent. They were later found burned and suffocated in the ashes and debris. In all, twenty-five people were killed in Ludlow.

John D. Rockefeller, a part owner of the mine, was held responsible for what became known as the Ludlow Massacre. The incident caused a national outcry, and protests were organized across the country. Demonstrations at Rockefeller's mansion near Tarrytown, New York, became increasingly violent, and several individuals, including Berg, were arrested, along with future coconspirator Arthur Caron, a member of the Industrial Workers of the World. The atrocities in Colorado caused one of the most famous battles over free speech to take place in the courts and streets of Tarrytown at the time. The Colorado massacre and the Tarrytown battle enraged many radicals. Their anger was further enflamed when police attacked a May Day rally in Union Square, injuring and arresting a large number of protesters.[7]

Members of the Latvian Anarchist Red Cross (including Berg, Hanson, and Berger) and Italian anarchists from the Bresci Circle held secret meetings to discuss how to respond to the escalation of brutality by the state and capitalists. They, along with other sympathetic anarchists, secretly began to make arrangements to bomb Rockefeller's mansion.[8] Several meetings were held at the Ferrer Center, where they devised a plan in which Caron, Berg, and Hanson would plant a bomb at Rockefeller's home in Tarrytown. For reasons unknown, the plan was called off at the last moment and the three men returned to Berger's apartment from Tarrytown, with the bomb in hand.

According to eyewitnesses, the three men along with Alexander Berkman met once more that night at the Ferrer Center to discuss further plans. According to some of those individuals involved in the plot, Berkman was the chief conspirator but chose to remain behind the scenes of the plot rather than on the front line.[9] Despite claims by others, Berkman denied any involvement or knowledge of the plan. The meeting went late into the night and the men decided to make a second attempt at Rockefeller the next morning.

THE EXPLOSION

At 9:00 a.m. on July 4, Louise Berger left her apartment and headed to the office of the anarchist paper *Mother Earth* on 119th Street. Some have speculated she was heading to the office to inform Berkman that the bomb had been readjusted and was ready.[10] Other accounts suggest that she was told to stay away from the apartment the night before and was never at the apartment on the morning of the explosion.

At 9:16 a.m., an explosion occurred in the seven-story tenement at 1626 Lexington Avenue. The three upper floors of the tenement building were wrecked from the blast. Debris and rubble showered the rooftops and the streets of the heavily immigrant-populated area of Harlem. Large pieces of furniture were thrown hundreds of feet in the air due to the power of the blast.

The bomb intended for Rockefeller exploded prematurely, killing four (Carl Hanson, Charles Berg, Arthur Caron, and Marie Chavez). Investigators suggested that since Hanson was blown to pieces and Berg's head and feet were blown off that perhaps Hanson was holding the bomb as Berg was attaching the bomb to an electrical detonator when it went off. However, Joseph Cohen, a former member of the Philadelphia Anarchist Red Cross who had moved to New York just seven months prior to the explosion, claimed that the bomb was stashed under one of the beds and that perhaps some in the apartment were engaging in horseplay, unaware of tragic events that would be set off by their actions.[11]

Regardless of what triggered the explosion the blast did significant damage. Berg's body was found pinned against the wall by debris. Spectators witnessed pieces of Hanson's body being thrown into the street and onto the roof of a nearby church.[12] The blast threw Caron onto the mangled and twisted fire escape. The body of Marie Chavez was found mutilated in the apartment. Chavez, twenty-eight years old, had not been involved in the conspiracy but merely rented an apartment adjoined to the one that had exploded. In total, twenty other people were injured, seven of them severely enough to be hospitalized.[13]

Another man, a Wobbly named Mike Murphy, had spent the night in the apartment. When the explosion occurred, his bed fell into the apartment below. Slightly dazed and confused, Murphy was able to walk away from the incident with only the loss of some clothes and a few minor bruises. Supposedly, Murphy was unaware of either the plan or that there had been so much explosive material in the apartment. During the chaos after the bombing, police took Murphy to the police station where they gave him some old clothes. Murphy was able to slip away to the *Mother Earth* headquarters, where Berkman quickly sent him away accompanied by Charles Plunkett, another coconspirator. Murphy was first taken to Westfield, New Jersey, and then to Philadelphia by members of the Radical Library and finally on to Canada. He eventually moved to England and never returned to the United States.[14]

Allegedly, another Wobbly, Isidore Wisotsky, was present in the apartment but was blown out by the force of the explosion.[15] Wisotsky, who was involved in the unemployment movement, was never connected directly with the plot. He survived the blast.

On the day of the accident, a member of the Bresci group, Frank Mandese, was arrested in close proximity to Rockefeller's home in Tarrytown. With a lack of evidence, the police were forced to release him. Soon afterwards, the police raided the Bresci Circle and roughed up its members, whom they suspected were involved in the bomb plot against Rockefeller, though they had little proof.

THE AFTERMATH

The incident caused immediate repercussions against the Ferrer Center. Police agents infiltrated the adult classes to detect any remaining coconspirators of Hanson, Berg, and Caron. The center acquired a reputation as a bomb factory and a hotbed for subversion. Support for the center dwindled to such an extent that the collective was later forced to move outside New York City and begin again in Stelton.[16]

Despite the increased repression caused by the incident, anarchists remained loyal to their comrades, hailing them as heroes. Poems written by Mike Gold and Adolf Wolff were published in *Di Shtime fun di rusishe gefangene*, the newspaper of the Russian section of the Anarchist Red Cross, and Emma Goldman's *Mother Earth*.

The following was Wolff's poem written in memory of his fallen comrades:

Arthur Caron, Charles Berg, Charles Hanson

The mammoth beast whose name is ignorance
And all its brood of venom-spitting cubs
In chorus hiss and howl their hellish glee
Over the death of our martyred comrades.

But in this world can greater glory be
Than to be hated by the powers of darkness?
To be misunderstood and crucified
Has ever been the fate of those who fought
The fight of light against the powers of darkness.

Ye hordes of knaves and fools, the day will come
When your descendants, shamed to call you sires,
Will raise a monument unto these men
Over whose torn remains you sneering gloat.[17]

Detectives rounded up associates of the three dead anarchists including Alexander Berkman and Louise Berger. Berger claimed she had no knowledge of any plot or bomb-making material in her apartment. After the interrogation she was taken to the morgue, where she identified the mangled remains of Hanson and Berg.[18]

Berkman only admitted that the men were anarchists and that he had met with them and others who had been arrested in Tarrytown. He was then also taken to the morgue to identify the dead. Later Berkman and Louise Berger were able to obtain the bodies of their comrades for cremation and a funeral demonstration at Union Square. The authorities refused to allow a public funeral to take place for the anarchists. Regardless, their friends were insistent that a funeral of their beloved comrades and a rally would take place.[19]

THE FUNERAL

On July 11, supporters gathered in Union Square several hours before the scheduled rally. The police held on to their position that they would not allow the funeral and rally to continue, but instead of attempting to remove the crowd from Union Square, detectives arrived at Berkman's house to seize the urn that contained the remains of the three men.

One step ahead of the police, Berkman was able to slip out the back door where he had an automobile waiting for him. He sped toward the demonstration in hopes of being able to make it to the speaking podium before being caught. As he approached the crowd, the police mistook Berkman's bright red car to be that of the Fire Chief and eagerly cleared a lane for the car all the way up to the speaker stand, made from two huge dry goods boxes. By the time the police realized what had transpired, Berkman was already into his speech. Any attempt to seize Berkman or the urn at this point would have caused a riot.[20]

One by one, anarchists and sympathizers took to the platform and gave praise to the three dead men while at the same time condemning Rockefeller and the capitalist system. Alexander Berkman, Carlos Tresca, Elizabeth Gurley Flynn, Leonard Abbott and a dozen others spoke to the crowd of approximately 5,000 about the lives of the three men and their struggle for justice and love for humanity.

The crowd was dressed in red and black to mourn the deaths of Berg, Caron, and Hanson. Men wore a red rose in the lapels of their coats, while women decorated their hats, necks, and arms with red ribbons. Those in the crowd took their hats off in respect every time the names of three men were mentioned in the fiery speeches.

After the demonstration, the urn was placed in the offices of *Mother Earth*, which had been decorated with wreaths and black and red banners. The bronze urn, which rested on a red cloth-covered altar, took the shape of a pyramid with a clenched fist reaching out of its apex. Inside the pyramid were three compartments, each containing the ashes of one of the three anarchists.[21]

The creator of the urn, Adolf Wolff, explained the meaning of the design:

> It conveys three meanings. By the pyramid is indicated the present unjust gradation of society into classes, with the masses on the bottom and the

privileged classes towering above them to the apex, where the clenched fist, symbolical of the social revolution, indicates the impending vengeance of those free spirits who refuse to be bound by the present social system and rise above it, threatening its destruction. The urn further symbolizes the strength and endurance of the revolution in so solid a base. A third suggestion is that of a mountain in the course of eruption, the crude, misshapen stern fist indicating the lava of human indignation which is about to belch forth and carry destruction to the volcano which has given it birth.[22]

Years later, with the deaths of Sacco and Vanzetti in 1927, Wolff was called forward to design the urn that would hold their ashes. The urn was an emulation of his earlier design for the victims of the Lexington Avenue explosion. The replication of the design did not take away from the powerful impression felt by the viewers of the urn.[23]

Thousands of mourners passed through the offices of *Mother Earth* to pay their last respects for Berg, Caron, and Hanson. After the funeral, the urn was taken to the Ferrer Center where it remained until the school closed several years later. The ashes were taken to Central Park and were scattered by the boys from the Ferrer Center.[24] Afterwards, the bronze fist and hollowed pyramid of the urn were sent to the Stelton colony, an anarchist commune in New Jersey that was established out of the Ferrer Center. The urn was used as a bell to call children and adults to meetings.[25]

As for Louise Berger, the death of her beloved comrades and stepbrother did not deter her from her revolutionary passion. In 1917, like many revolutionaries, she traveled to Russia to participate in creating the new society.

In January 1918, in response to the US arrest and prosecution of labor radicals Thomas Mooney and Warren Billings for the 1916 Preparedness Day bombing, armed sailors and anarchists from Petrograd marched to the American embassy to arrest the American ambassador in Russia. He was threatened that he would be held hostage until the release of both Mooney and Billings, as well as Alexander Berkman. Berkman was arrested in June 1917 and sentenced to two years in federal prison under the Espionage Act of 1917 for encouraging young men not to register for the draft. During the confrontation with the ambassador over the plight of the three men, Louise Berger served as an interpreter. The ambassador sent a telegram to Washington and promised to help secure the release of the imprisoned men.[26]

Despite being in Russia, the United States continued to view Louise Berger as a threat and danger. When the Galleani bombing campaign began, the Bureau of Investigation shifted their attention to the whereabouts of Berger. Since the Lexington explosion, she was given the unfortunate nickname "Dynamite Louise" by the media and government. The bureau now believed that Berger may have been involved in the Galleani bombing that targeted Judge Nott's home in June 1919.[27] Despite knowing that Berger had left for Russia during the outbreak of the Russian Revolution, government agents searched throughout the country and on all outgoing steamships for Louise Berger to ensure she didn't flee after the bombing. However, she never returned to the US and remained in Russia where she took part in bank expropriations in Odessa. It is believed that she died in the typhus epidemic a few years later.[28]

ARTICLE ANNOUNCING THE REVIVAL OF THE NEW YORK ANARCHIST RED CROSS

The following article, written by members of the Red Cross explaining its reasoning for its reappearance, was published in the anarchist journal *Freedom* in May 1923.—Ed.

THE ANARCHIST RED CROSS IN THE USA

Comrades,

The Anarchist Red Cross has been reorganized and we therefore give a brief review explaining the causes for such reorganization.

From 1909 to 1917 the Anarchist Red Cross was active in the aiding both morally and financially the captives of the Russian Tsar in Siberia, Schlusselburg, etc. The Russian Revolution in 1917 spread new hope for a better world. The news that all the political prisoners were freed and were met by the Russian people as their brothers, with fraternal love and understanding, brought our comrades to the realization that their mission was at an end and that, instead of helping prisoners, their place was among the revolutionary workers and peasants, on the streets and in the cities of the country which sent out a call to the entire world—a call of freedom. But the freedom did not last long.

At the end of 1917 the Communist Party gained power by adopting the prevailing motto they forgot as soon as they got into power, and liberty-loving idealists, who foresaw a new autocracy in the aims of the Communist Party, and who stated it openly, were thrown into jail by the new rulers and sent to Siberia, to Archangel, etc.

Among the thousands of political prisoners there were hundreds of Anarchists, men and women, who were brutally tortured by the servants of the Cheka for protesting against their unjust imprisonment. Among these Anarchists were very young people who had just begun to work in the revolutionary movement, but most of them were the pioneers of the movement, who gave all they possessed, their very lives, to the cause of the Social Revolution, which was stopped by the new autocratic government of Russia.

Today, under Communist rulership, captives of the new regime are being tortured in the very same dungeons from which they were freed only five years ago by the Russian people. A notable exception is the fortress of St. Peter and Paul, which has been converted into a museum for exhibition to foreign visitors. The new rulers have devised new schemes for torturing prisoners, with which those of the ancient fortress cannot complete. Thousands of men and women are kept in the heavily barred prisons throughout the length and breadth of Russia. From Kiev to Vladivostok and from Odessa to Archangel, the cries of our comrades are being silenced by death.

The aim of the Anarchist Red Cross is to help these and other comrades who are imprisoned for their ideas in every part of the world. We therefore call upon you to assist us in our task morally and financially, and we hope you will do your utmost to let our comrades in prison know that we outside are doing all in our power to comfort them.

The Anarchist Red Cross

Address all correspondence to Y. Firer, care of *Freie Arbeiter Stimme*, 48 Canal Street, New York City, USA.

CORRESPONDENCE BETWEEN LILLIE SARNOFF AND ALEXANDER BERKMAN

The following correspondence is between Lillie Sarnoff and Alexander Berkman. Lillie Sarnoff was a member of the New York Anarchist Red Cross. Alexander Berkman had recently fled from Russia and was working with the Joint Committee for the Defense of the Revolutionaries Imprisoned in Russia. The topic of this correspondence is whether anarchist aid groups should collaborate with non-anarchist organizations to support anarchist and non-anarchist prisoners. It is important to understand that the Joint Committee was created by members of the Society to Aid Imprisoned Anarchists, a group that succeeded the Anarchist Black Cross in Russia. It was formed to continue the work of the Black Cross after its members were arrested for prison support. The Joint Committee collaborated with other organizations whose members were suffering the same conditions as the anarchists inside Russia.

Another issue raised in this correspondence is how Berkman uses his influence and the impact that has on other aid organizations working toward the same or similar goals.—Ed.

LILLIE SARNOFF'S LETTER TO ALEXANDER BERKMAN, JUNE 28, 1924:

Dear Comrade B.,

I received your two letters with the Statement. I will try to send that 2nd Bulletin this week. I cannot now write of other various news, but there are a few vital things to be written so I'll write them now without more ado.

First, most of the news you write here, is already know to us. We not merely know—but are already actually in touch with them—such as "Annie." We had already sent her money when your letter came. To that comrade who is to visit Solevetsky we also had already sent some money—only a smaller amount than to you. So it seems we are in touch with the same people you are. . . .

Of course, you know our stand—(this is in re: the withdrawing of the Russian comrades from the Joint Committee). It has always been and is still against working jointly. That is the reason, as you well know, that we always stipulate when we send money, that it is to go solely for the Anarchists, so that the money should not go through the Joint Committee. Anarchists and Social Rev. cannot work together. That meeting for June 6th was never held. The Social Rev. were to have called it and didn't—as they do but little work—and this thing fell through as have many other things. The FAS, wanted to go in to work with them on that meeting and they refused—and that shows too—their spirit of cooperation.

Now there is another important matter that it seems must be thrashed out well, before any other work can go on between you and us (ARC). You know our work. You know that we are trying to raise money in all ways that we can and use it for the sole purpose of helping Anarchist prisoners.

You know too that we are not one—or a few—but a group—a group, which could with proper help and cooperation expand and grow so that other groups in different parts of the country could be formed and cooperate together with us. However, whether you realize it or not, and I don't suppose you really do (that is why we are explaining this) you are really, instead of aiding us—hindering our work. This is how that happens. You send out letters to different people all over the country with *your name* only—quite ignoring our (ARC) existence—and ask for help. You being well known, people send money to you (through the FAS). Now if in those letters you spoke of us—that we are doing this work—with you—if you referred them to us, saying that we would send the money to you, since we are an organized body, working expressly for the purpose of helping prisoners, a much different and better result would be. Now people send in money direct to you—and if they think of the Red Cross at all, it may be perhaps to wonder what we [do], since you are collecting money for that purpose. I've tried to make this as clear as I could, and I believe you understand. If the RC and you are to continue to cooperate we must do this on a cooperating basis from *both* sides—that you must recognize us—publicly—in your letters, appeals, etc., as well as merely to receive money from us to send to people, many of whom we are already in touch with.

I am not trying to make the matter seem worse than it is. This is how I have been authorized to write by the group, and as I see it. This is not quite right that while we are trying in all ways to collect money, that you send appeals and letters *in your name*, as if we had no existence at all. If I could read Jewish, I would cut out the clipping of the FAS for you—to see how bad that is—ARC announcing their regular meetings, etc., and money being sent direct to you printed in the same other another page [*sic*]. Perhaps some comrades will send these clipping to you—or I believe you must have that paper yourself —and can look it over.

Now please consider this thoroughly, Comrade B.— what you think and how you wish to act. We shall wait for your reply to consider what next steps to take. Of course if, comradely, you wished to cooperate with us we believe that both the Red Cross and the treasury holding the money to go for our imprisoned comrades would greatly improve. But we can work it out more fully later. Now, we will wait to hear your reply to this.

Fraternally,
Lillie Sarnoff

ALEXANDER BERKMAN'S RESPONSE TO LILLIE SARNOFF, DATED JULY 22, 1924:

Dear Comrade Sarnoff:

Your letter of June 28 (written by you in the name of your group) and copies of the Bulletin #2 received. This reply is to you as well as to the comrades of the [Anarchist] Red Cross.

You know my position in regard to aid of the revolutionists imprisoned in Russia. As I said in the statement recently issued by myself and Mark Mratchny, I do not consider aid to imprisoned revolutionists in the light of political work. It is not necessary here to repeat all that I said in the statement, a copy of which I sent to you.

To me, in this connection, supplying bread to a Maria Spiridonovna (who is a Left Socialist-Revolutionary) is just as imperative as to aid A. Baron (who is an anarchist). It is not a question of the political views of the prisoners. It is enough for me that they are sincere revolutionists.

Concerning your remark that we cannot work with Left SRs, I may tell you that we, at least I, could also not work together with many of the anarchists who are in the prisons of the Bolsheviki. Yet I am willing to help them, as prisoners. Among the anarchists in prison are many individualists, Stirnerians, Universalists, Gordinists, (who are worse than crazy), etc., etc. Some among them are pure cranks who did us more harm than good in the revolution. Yet you even send help to all anarchists, not asking what their particular views and opinions are. Some of those "anarchists" cannot even be considered as anarchists in our sense, yet we are willing to help all of them. I can assure you that as a revolutionist I felt nearer [to] Spiridonovna, Kamkov, or Trutovsky (I knew them all personally and spent many days with them in Moscow) than to some of those individualists and Stirnerians who you are willing—and justly—to regard as anarchists. In short, I would help Sophia Perovskaya and Zheliabov in prison, the same way as I would help Baron or Meier-Rubinchik. (If you really wanted to carry out your view logically, you should aid *only* anarchist-communists in prison, for the Universalists, for instance, are as far from us as the Left SRs and perhaps even farther in points of ideas.)

As a matter of fact, the anarchists in the prisons of Russia *share* the things they receive with the Left SRs, and the latter do the same. Among revolutionists in prison political distinctions are abolished so far as food etc. is concerned. You will therefore realize how stupid it is of the fellow in the New York, *Izvestia*, who asked me whether I would also "work with Denikin and Wrangel to aid their prisoners." We are speaking of revolutionists in prison, not of counter-revolutionists. To me the Left SRs are revolutionists, even if I disagree with their political view.

Well, you are at liberty to have your own opinion in the matter. That is why I call myself an anarchist, leaving others free to act and think as they believe best. but at the same time, I claim the right for myself to act as I think proper under given circumstances.

Now, you surprise me when you speak of cooperation. I have not noticed any on your part. Two years ago, when I started to publish my pamphlet on Russia, which I considered important to spread the truth about the Bolsheviki, I appealed to you and your—the group—promised to cooperate. I have never heard another word from you or the group about it. It was the lack of cooperation in that work that forced me to suspend the series which was to consist of ten or twelve pamphlets.

As to the money you sent, I merely served for you as a medium through which you forwarded funds to Russia. This cooperation was on *my* side.

You speak of a letter that I sent out in *my own name* to get help for Russia. I claim that right to do so, of course. But as a matter of fact, all such work is done by the Joint Committee and its name. It is only occasionally, to some personal friends (whom I can reach better than the Committee) that I send a personal letter. Such cases are very rare, because of all that I did long ago, when I stood alone in this work, immediately after I left Russia. Already in Riga I sent out the first appeal, almost 3 years ago. And that also was *not* in my own name but was signed by Shapiro and E.G. as well as myself.

I know that some people and groups send money directly here instead of to you. For instance, Volin and his group often receive funds for Russia. Some are also received by the Joint Committee, also Kater and often also by R. Rocker. Sometime also funds are sent directly to me. For instance, an Italian group in Chicago sent some recently. Also I recently received funds from *Freie Arb. Stimme* (for Russia), which the *Stimme* received from some St. Louis comrades whom I even don't know, nor do I know the Italian group in Chicago, etc. In other words, people send funds *as they please.* Most of these people and groups probably don't even know of your existence, or some of them may prefer to send funds to others, not you. Surely that is not my fault.

I, personally, am indifferent as to where and how people send help to Russia. I am only interested in seeing that our prisoners should receive aid. *How* and *by whom* is just the same, just so that they get it.

This is about all there is to be said on the subject. I have explained my position to you, and I hope that you clearly understand it.

Fraternally
AB

NOTES

FOREWORD

1   "Bessie Yelensky 1891–1968," *Freedom* (London) 29, no 7 (November 30, 1968).

2   Federal Bureau of Investigation (FBI), Old German Files, 1909–21, Morris Burstein (#202600-2524-1).

3   "Police Control Jobless Quarter," *Chicago Daily Tribune*, January 29, 1914.

4   FBI, Old German Files, 1909–21, Morris Burstein (#202600-2524-1).

5   FBI, Bureau Section Files, 1909–21, Albert Bailin (#43–33).

6   FBI, Bureau Section Files, 1909–21, Albert Bailin (#43–33); Federal Bureau of Investigation. Bureau Section Files, 1909–21, Albert Bailin (#202600-96).

7   FBI, Old German Files, 1909–21, Jake Goodman (#318106); FBI, Old German Files, 1909–21. Various (#8000-160053).

8   FBI, Old German Files, 1909–21, Various (#228898).

9   FBI, Old German Files, 1909–21, European Neutrality Matters. Morris Waisman (#52632).

10 FBI, Old German Files, 1909–21, Anarchist Activities (#370313).

11 Paul Avrich, *The Russian Anarchists* (Princeton: Princeton University Press, 1967), 222.

12 Barry Pateman, "Cries in the Wilderness: Alexander Berkman and Russian Prisoner Aid," in *Bloodstained: One Hundred Years of Leninist Counterrevolution*, ed. Friends of Aron Baron (Chico: AK Press, 2017), 248.

13 Alexander Berkman (contributor), *The Tragic Procession: Alexander Berkman and Russian Prisoner Aid* (Berkeley: Alexander Berkman Social Club, 2020), vii–ix.

14 Chris Ealham, *Living Anarchist: José Peirats and the Spanish Anarchist Movement* (Oakland: AK Press, 2016), 191.

15 Alicia Berta Quintero Maqua, "The Echo of the Prisoners: Libertarians

in Franco's Prisons and Solidarity Outside the Prisons, 1936–1963" (PhD thesis, University of Madrid, 2016), 341.

16 Maqua, "Echo," 346.

17 Maqua, "Echo," 347.

18 Maqua, "Echo," 348–49.

19 Stuart Christie, *Edward Heath Made Me Angry* (Hastings, UK: Christie Books, 2004), 61.

20 *Bulletin of the Anarchist Black Cross* 1, no. 7 (January 1970): 3–5.

21 *Bulletin*, 3–5.

22 *Bulletin*, 3–5.

23 *Bulletin*, 6.

24 *Frankfurter Gemeine* (Frankfurt Community), no. 6 (November 1972), 3; *Befreiung*, April 1972, 23.

25 *Black Flag* 3, no. 1 (March 1973), 7; *Befreiung* (January–March 1972), 3–4; *Heinzel Press*, no.6 (1972), 4.

26 *Freedom* 37, no. 7 (April 3, 1976), 3; *Libertarian Struggle* (September 1975), 5.

27 Christie, *Edward Heath*, 118.

28 Bommi Baumann, *How It All Began* (Vancouver, BC: Pulp Press, 1981), 79–84.

29 *Arbeiterkampf* 1, no 23 (December 1971), 4.

30 Albert Meltzer, *The International Revolutionary Solidarity Movement: First of May Group* (Orkney Islands: Cienfuegos Press, 1976), 81; Michael Sontheimer, "Nachruf auf Bommi Baumann: Wie alles endete," *Die Tageszeitung*, July 20, 2016, https://taz.de/Nachruf-auf-Bommi-Baumann/!5320956.

31 *Black Flag* 1, no 2 (November 1, 1968).

32 *Freedom* 35, no. 16 (April 20, 1973), 1.

33 *Freedom* 37, no. 12 (June 26, 1976), 1.

34 Liam Collins, "Murdered in the Line of Duty by a Married Couple in a Dublin Park," *Irish Independent*, September 10, 2022, https://www.independent.ie/irish-news/murdered-in-the-line-of-duty-by-a-married-couple-in-a-dublin-park/41979411.html.

35 Christie, *Edward Heath*, 17; "Police See Letter on Embassy Shooting," *The Guardian*, August 23, 1967.

36 Christie, *Edward Heath*, 89–93.

37 Meltzer, *International Revolutionary Solidarity Movement*, 73–74.

38 "Police Hunt for 'Bomb Attack' Man," *Birmingham Post*, January 15, 1971.

39 C.A. Coughlin, "Bombs at Carr Home 'Work of Anarchists,'" *Daily Telegraph*, November 11, 1971; C.A. Coughlin, "Prescott Gets 15 Years for 'Evil Conspiracy,'" *Daily Telegraph*, December 2, 1971.

40 "Angry Brigade Case Verdict," *Evening Standard*, December 2, 1972.

41 Christie, *Edward Heath*, 260–61.

42 Christie, *Edward Heath*, 261–62.

43 Christie, *Edward Heath*, 270; *Black Flag: Organ of the Anarchist Black Cross* 4, no. 9 (July 1976).

44 Albert Meltzer, *I Couldn't Paint Golden Angels* (Oakland: AK Press, 1996), 278–80.

45 "Verdict in Arms Case Questioned," *Daily Telegraph*, December 20, 1979.

46 "Bungling Raiders Jailed for Seven Years," *Black County Evening Mail*, December 23, 1977, 16.

47 *Black Flag* 5, no. 7 (1978–January 1979); Stuart Christie, *Christie Files*, (Orkney Islands: Cienfuegos Press 1980), 351.

48 "Jail Ordeal Over—Former Honley Woman Relaxes," *Huddersfield Daily Examiner*, June 1, 1981, 3.

49 *ABC Bulletin*, no. 1; *Black Flag* 2, no. 12 (June 1972).

50 *Phoenix Rising* 8, no. 2 (May 1989).

51 *Black Flag*, no. 179 (February 1988).

52 *Black Flag*, no. 191 (May 1989); *Black Flag*, no. 192 (July 1989).

53 *Ecomedia Bulletin*, no. 69, (January–February 1990).

54 *Jersey Anarchist*, no. 22 (November 1994).

55 Berkman to Lillie Sarnoff, July 22, 1924, Alexander Berkman Papers, Inventory Number Arch00040.8, International Institute of Social History, Amsterdam.

56 Rodolfo Montes De Oca, "Nucleos De Libertad: 4 Entrevistas a Diferentes CNS/ABC del Mundo," *Liberlos Abolicionistas*, no. 2.

57 Lorenzo Kom'boa Ervin, *A New Draft Proposal for an Anarchist Black Cross Network* (Fordsburg: Zabalaza Press, 2002), 7.

58 *Jersey Anarchist*, no. 3 (October 1992): 1.

59 *Jersey Anarchist*, no. 12 (September 1993): 1.

60 *Claustrophobia*, no. 7 (Spring 1996): 3.

61 "FBI Places City Man on Most-Wanted List," *Asbury Park Press*, October 19, 1989.

62 Robert S. Mueller III, "Senate Committee on Intelligence of the United States Senate, February 16, 2005, Washington, DC, https://archives.fbi.gov/archives/news/testimony/global-threats-to-the-u.s.-and-the-fbis-response-1.

63 FBI, Matthew Hart (#1445554-000).

64 "Lawmakers Seek Probe of N.J. Cops' Steroid Use," *Press of Atlantic City*, December 15, 2010; "Docs Focus of Steroid Probe: Feds Subpoena data on Prescriptions," *Herald-News*, May 8, 2011; Ammy Brittain and Mark Mueller, "Strong at Any Cost: Legal Cases Linked to N.J. Police Who Received Steroid Through Dr. Coloa," *Star Ledger*, December 12, 2010, https://www.nj.com/news/2010/12/strong_at_any_cost_legal_cases.html.

65 *Daily Record*, February 4, 2010.

66 Mueller, "Senate Committee on Intelligence of the United States Senate."

67 Michele McPhee, "FBI: Anarchists Operating a Hub," *Boston Herald*, February 28, 2005; *El Libertario*, no. 45 (November 2004–January 2005); *Cette Semaine*. no. 88 (March 2006).

68 *ABCF Update*, no. 49 (Winter 2008); *Freedom*, September 4, 2005.

69   *El Libertario*, no. 45 (November 2004–January 2005); *El Libertario*, no. 43 (June–July 2005).

70   *Bruchstellen*, no. 24 (October 2016).

71   *Bruchstellen*, no. 65 (December 2020).

72   *Black Flag*, no. 220 (2001): 7; *Green Anarchy*, no. 5 (Spring 2005): 7.

73   *Resistance*, no. 23 (March 2001); *Onward* 2, no. 1, 16.

74   *Direct Action*, no. 6 (2004): 6.

75   *Enterao*, no. 67 (September 2002): 21–24.

76   *La Burxa*, no. 55 (September 2002).

77   *Enterao*, no. 67 (September 2002): 21–24.

78   *Do or Die*, no. 10, 292.

79   *El Libertario*, no. 45 (November 2004–January 2005); *El Libertario*, no. 43 (June–July 2005).

80   *El Quijote*, no. 692 (November 24, 2014): 37.

81   *Fenrir*, no. 6, 4.

82   *Atentados*, no. 8 (June 2015).

83   *Autonomy*, no. 35 (December 2013).

84   "Russia Expels Finnish Anarchist After Protests," *Agence France Presse— English*, April 5, 2012.

85   "Russia Lists Anarchist Black Cross as 'Undesirable Organisation,'" *BBC Monitoring Former Soviet Union—Political Supplied by BBC Worldwide Monitoring*, February 19, 2024.

II   THE 1905 REVOLUTION

1   The Political Red Cross is known to have existed as early as 1872. However, the formation existed in connection with specific political parties, such as the Zemlia i Volia (Land and Liberty) and then later with the Narodnaya Volya (People's Will). It not only raised funds for those in prison and in exile but was also known to have organized escape attempts for those it supported. The organization also helped young women escape from parental restraints by organizing fictitious marriages for them. In 1881, a foreign section of the Political Red Cross was established by a joint effort from the Narodnaya Volya and the Chernyi Peredel (Black Repartition). It was during this period in this formation that the Political Red Cross's goal was to provide nonpartisan aid to prisoners. However, political parties began to try to influence the work of the Political Red Cross and tensions between factions began to grow.—Ed.

2   Vera Figner was released from Strelnikov Prison in late 1904. She was exiled and banned from traveling until 1906. After the ban was lifted, she traveled Europe speaking on behalf of political prisoners, but there is no record of her visit to London until 1909. Between June and August of 1907, the Russian Social Revolutionary Party did have a series of conferences in London and Stuttgart, Germany. It is possible that Figner's attendance in London was unreported or that the conversation took place in Stuttgart. In either case, it is known that the Anarchist

Red Cross was formed in London before October 1907. By this time the ARC was already active in Russia. In 1906–7, five members of the Anarchist Red Cross were put on trial along with 162 other anarchists. Anarchist Red Cross chapters were known to exist in Odessa, Kiev, Bialystok, and other cities. As mentioned in this book, Harry Weinstein, one of the founders of the ARC in Russia, was detained in July or August 1906. It was after his release that the organization was allegedly formed. We know that he had been living in the United States by May 1907. With the information available to us, we can hypothesize that the ARC in Russia began during the period of July 1906 to May 1907. Internationally, it began during the summer of 1907.—Ed.

3   Harry Weinstein was active in the anarchist movement in Bialystok before being arrested in 1906. He immigrated to the United States in May 1907. He worked in the textile industry where he would become involved in the International Ladies' Garment Workers. Weinstein also acted as the treasurer of the New York Anarchist Red Cross.—Ed.

4   Jacob Katzenelenbogen was a Russian-born anarchist. He was active in the anarchist movement in Bialystok before immigrating to the United States in 1906. According to the 1910 census, he worked as a cigar maker.—Ed.

5   Weitzman was the alias for Morris Ganberg. He became an anarchist around the time of the 1905 Revolution in Russia. After the police raided his apartment, Ganberg traveled to Argentina and then immigrated to the United States in 1910. He resumed his activities in the movement, joining the New York chapter of the ARC. He returned to Russia after the 1917 Revolution where he fought against the White Army with Sholem Schwartzbard's anarchist detachment. He eventually returned to the United States. He resumed his anarchist activities in New York, serving many years on the Executive Board of *Freie Arbeiter Stimme.*—Ed.

6   Iza (Isador) Wishniak (also spelled "Wishnack"), along with his wife Fanny Wishniak, were active members of the New York Anarchist Red Cross. Iza was active in the anarchist movement in Bialystok and was sentenced to Siberian exile. He immigrated to the United States around 1908 after being released from prison in Russia. Fanny Wishniak, (née Alpert), emigrated from Poland around 1910. Based on census documents Iza was a boarder with Fanny's family before they married. Both worked in the garment industry. Besides the Anarchist Red Cross, the two were involved in various political organization, including the Workmen's Circle.—Ed.

7   Barukh (Bernard) Yelin was born in 1891 in Bialystok, Russia. He became active in the anarchist movement and was eventually imprisoned for his actions. Yelin immigrated to the United States where he became active in the anarchist movement and became the secretary of the ILGWU Local 35. Yelin eventually met Fannie Wexler, an anarchist active in Philadelphia. The two moved to Los Angeles in the 1930s,

where they became active in the Kropotkin Literary Society, Branch 413 of the Workmen's Circle. This organization would later help to organize the Arestantin Balls in Los Angeles as late as 1932. The group would also organize picnics and other fundraisers to collect money for aid to anarchists in Europe.—Ed.

8 The concert was held at the Grand Manhattan Hall on Grand Street. The concert was overflowing, and a number of those in attendance participated in the official launching of the Anarchist Red Cross in New York a few months later.—Ed.

9 Morris Beresin (also spelled Berezin) was a Russian-Jewish anarchist active in the Russian anarchist movement during the 1905 Revolution. He was sentenced to a Siberian labor camp in 1906. He eventually escaped and came to the United States around 1912. He settled for a time in Philadelphia where he joined the Radical Library and helped to form the Anarchist Red Cross chapter. While in Philadelphia he wrote a book, *From Chains to Freedom: Notes from a Fugitive Political Hard-Labor Convict*, which was published by the Anarchist Red Cross in 1916. He eventually moved to Baltimore where he was active in the Union for Russian Workers. In 1921, he was arrested during the Palmer Raids, where he dealt with the threat of deportation. He returned to Philadelphia until his passing in February 1971.—Ed.

10 *Die Stimme* (the correct title was *Di Shtime fun di Rusishe Gefangene*) was a monthly publication from 1913 to 1916. It was edited by Alexander Zager.—Ed.

III RELIEF IN THE USA, 1908–17

1 The London Anarchist Red Cross started in 1907 under the direction of Peter Kropotkin, Rudolf Rocker, Alexander Schapiro, and Cherkezov. The group in London also produced a journal known as the *Hilf-Ruf* (The Call to Aid)—*Organ of the Anarchist Red Cross* during 1911–12. It was written half in Yiddish and half in Russian. Like the other groups in the United States, the London chapter organized Arestantin Balls for anarchist prisoners, organizing them as late as 1924. In addition to aid for anarchist prisoners, the London Anarchist Red Cross raised funds for other causes. In December 1913, the group organized a ball to raise funds for the "Dublin Kiddies' Fund." (*Daily Herald*, December 23, 1913.)—Ed.

2 According to *Dielo Truda*, Anarchist Red Cross chapters were established in New York (1909), Philadelphia (1911), Detroit (1914), Cincinnati (1914), Brownsville (1913), St. Louis (1913), and Chicago (1909) (*Dielo Truda*, no. 101). *Dielo Truda* does have the Philadelphia chapter as forming in 1911, but the letterhead used by the Philadelphia chapter during the same period places the year as 1912. A short-lived Milwaukee chapter was also formed in July 1916, but did not last more than a year. It is believed the Baltimore group formed when Beresin moved to the city. A Rochester ARC was also formed in April 1916.—Ed.

3   The very first Arestantin Ball was held on May 1, 1910, at the Terrace Lyceum, located at 206 East Broadway. It was cosponsored with *Mother Earth*, the anarchist newspaper published by Emma Goldman. While there are no media reports regarding the first dance, there are some reports that describe the second annual dance, which took place on April 8, 1911, at the Manhattan Lyceum, located at 6-68 East 4th Street. According to the *New York Times,* more than five hundred people attended the event. The *New York Tribune* characterized it as more of "a Russian Nihilist affair rather than an anarchist affair" and assured the public that it was "not a meeting of so-called professional anarchists." The ball became an annual event after moving over to the Harlem River Casino on 2nd Ave and 127th Street. The money that was raised typically went to support political prisoners in Russia, but the event also raised funds for the Mooney-Billings case and Milwaukee anarchists imprisoned for the 1917 police station bombing. ("Nihilist Dance to Aid Refugees," *New York Times*, April 9, 1911.)—Ed.

4   Anatoly Pokatiloff was a well-known Russian actor and helped to organize plays to raise funds for Russian aid organizations.—Ed.

5   A Milwaukee chapter formed on July 15, 1916. The Bouren Ball took place on December 2, 1916, at the Northside Auditorium on Eighth and Walnut. The following year, the Bureau of Investigation raided the home of Morris Waisman, a member of the Milwaukee chapter of the Anarchist Red Cross. Federal agents seized material, including material related to the activities of the local ARC.—Ed.

6   Prior to the formation of the Rochester ARC, anarchists in the city were raising funds for the Relief Society for Russian Political Prisoners until they received word that the anarchists in Russian prisons were not getting aid, despite the tremendous amount of effort the anarchist community spent raising funds for the organization. In response, the Rochester ARC was organized on April 12, 1916, with twenty-two members enrolled. Other ARC chapters not mentioned in this book were Boston (Dorchester), Cincinnati, St. Louis, Brownsville (Brooklyn), and the Lettish Anarchist Red Cross in New York.—Ed.

IV   THE KERENSKY PERIOD, 1917

1   One of the final tasks of the ARC was organizing and assisting anarchists' voyages back home. Volin has been mentioned in many texts as one of those assisted by the ARC on his trip back to Russia. The United States and Canada monitored the mass exodus of the Russian revolutionaries and were concerned about the "red" element that might be repatriating back to Russia. The governments expressed concern that the flooding of radicals back into Russia might negatively impact Russia in its hour of need, and there was a concern that those leaving for Russia advocated for a different peace process between Russia and Germany that might be a detriment to the allied forces in the war. FBI, Old German Files, 1909–21, Various (8000-19118).—Ed.

2   William Shatov (also spelled "Shatoff") was a member of the New York Anarchist Red Cross and worked on *Golos Truda*. He participated in the 1905 Revolution before coming to the United States in 1907. Although he claimed to have been a political prisoner while in the czarist prisons, members of the New York ARC were critical of these claims. Some argued he was nothing more than an "ordinary criminal" and "not an anarchist expropriator." Avrich, *Anarchist Voices*, 374. However, while in the United States, he helped to organize the Ferrer Modern School and the Union of Russian Workers. After his return to Russia, he and several other anarchists were part of the Petrograd Soviet's Military Revolutionary Committee that orchestrated the October Revolution. Shatov advocated for working with the Bolsheviks for the preservation of the Revolution and served in several governmental positions. Despite his willingness to cooperate, his anarchist beliefs still resulted in his arrest and execution during the Stalinist purges of the 1930s.—Ed.

3   When the members of the Anarchist Red Cross returned to Russia, they met up with many of the prisoners that they had supported. One such member of the organization, Morris Greenshner, traveled to Odessa after he arrived in Russia where he met up with Isaak Golovin, a person he had helped through his work in the ARC. Golovin embraced Greenshner, informing him that it was his letters that had kept him going through the years. He assisted Greenshner in getting a job at the factory where he was working. Another prisoner, Iosif Savitsky, heard that several members of the Anarchist Red Cross were in Odessa and traveled there in search of Greenshner in hopes of thanking him for what he had done for the one-time prisoner. Paul Avrich, *Anarchist Voices*, 378–80.—Ed.

V   BOLSHEVIK TRIUMPH

1   The attempted assassination of Lenin happened in August of 1918, four months after the raids against the anarchist newspaper and associated groups. The assassination attempt has been a common explanation used to legitimize the repression brought on against the anarchists by Lenin. This could hardly be an excuse for events that happened much earlier than the attempted assassination.—Ed.

2   On the night of April 12, 1918, the Cheka raided twenty-six anarchist centers in Moscow. Most of the anarchists surrendered without a fight, but many offered fierce resistance. By the end of the night, forty anarchists died, with over five hundred arrested. Most anarchist publications were suspended, and nearly all the leaders of the Moscow Federation of Anarchist Groups were arrested. Two days after the raids in Moscow, similar raids took place in Petrograd. Much like the previous raids, machine guns and cannons were trained upon the anarchist clubs as arrests took place. By April 20, most of the anarchists arrested during the raids had been released, but the government still detained close to fifty anarchists. According to the Bolsheviks, these raids were

done in the name of weeding out the criminal elements that hide within the anarchist movement. This excuse ignored the fact that the main targets of these raids were well-known anarchists.

Within a month, major anarchist newspapers, such as *Burevestnik*, *Anarkhiia*, and *Golos Truda*, were shut down by the Bolshevik government. At the same time, the government sent out a telegram calling for the disarming of all anarchist organizations. As in the past, the excuse of criminal elements within the anarchist movement was used as an excuse for this action. According to the telegram, "under the protective flag of Anarchist organizations operate thugs, thieves, gangsters, hold-up men and counter-revolutionists who are actively preparing to subvert the Soviet government." It seemed as though the Bolsheviks confused political opposition to the state with criminal behavior.—Ed.

3   This attack was done in response to the repression that took place after the attempted assassination of Lenin. However, the attack set off additional arrests and rationalized the Bolshevik repression of other revolutionary movements (Avrich, *Russian Anarchists*, 184–85).—Ed.

4   *Nabat* means the alarm bell or tocsin, which was rung in the Ukrainian villages to call urgent meetings of the community.

5   One of those who helped organize the Anarchist Black Cross was Apollon Karelin. Karelin was born in 1863 in St. Petersburg where he lived until 1881 when Czar Alexander II was assassinated. He was arrested for his involvement in the radical student movement and was sent to Peter-Paul fortress in Petersburg. After his release from prison, he joined the Populist Circles, which resulted in his continuous imprisonment. After the 1905 Revolution he fled to Paris where he started the Brotherhood of Free Communists. As with many revolutionaries, in 1917 he went back to Russia to assist the Revolution. In 1918, he became a soviet-anarchist and started an anarchist organization to persuade anti-Bolshevik anarchists to aid and help the communist government. In 1926, he died of a cerebral hemorrhage, but not before losing faith in the government, which arrested and banished most of his comrades into prisons.—Ed.

6   The manner in which the Black Cross manifested itself in the Ukraine was unique to the region. These Black Cross units were organized by Makhnovists, as both workers' self-defense units and medical units. The constant onslaughts by the pogromists, White Guard, and Red Army forced the city-dwellers to protect themselves from harm. It was the duty of the Black Cross to organize resistance against any actions brought on by their enemies. Although there was no specific uniform, during times of violence in the streets, a Black Cross member could be recognized by denim overalls and an arm band. As the White Guard became a threat, the Black Cross was often the only force in the town able to organize an immediate self-defense unit. Although they were able to properly defend their cities, they never became a mobile force like Makhno's army.—Ed.

7 In one situation, during the arrest of the secretariat of the anarchist groups of Ekaterinoslav, the Cheka confiscated over forty thousand rubles and clothes belonging to the Black Cross. The money seized by the Cheka was turned over to the State Bank, and the clothes were never returned.—Ed.

8 Along with the arrests of Makhno's army, members of the Nabat Federation were also arrested. Many of those were former members of the Anarchist Red Cross from the United States, and they would play decisive roles in the Taganka hunger strike.—Ed.

9 As the Kronstadt revolt waged on, Lenin seized the opportunity to rid himself of all opposition. He declared to the Tenth Party Congress, "The time has come, to put an end to opposition, to put a lid on it; we have had enough opposition." Following this statement, the Bolsheviks went on a rampage; arrests and killings of opposition groups took place all over the country. There was not a single industrial center or large settlement that remained free from sweeping arrests of groups in opposition to the Bolsheviks. Those who were arrested were either charged with "anti-Soviet propaganda," for promoting Menshevism, or for being a "counterrevolutionist." The arrest files of socialists and anarchist were emblazoned with the letters "C.R", or simply "counter-revolutionist" written in the file report. Included in these arrests were present or former members of the Anarchist Black Cross, including Yarchuk from the New York ARC and the infamous Gregory Maximoff (Avrich, *Russian Anarchists*, 229–32).—Ed.

10 Among those involved in the Taganka hunger strike were members of the ABC/ARC including Volin, Yarchuk, Mark Mratchny, and Maximoff. Olga Frydlin of the Anarchist Black Cross played a critical role in communicating the plight of the hunger strikers to those at the Red Trade Union Congress. She was allowed access to the anarchists because she was the spouse of Maximoff, allowing her to smuggle messages in and out of the prison.—Ed.

11 Emma Goldman and Alexander Berkman came to Russia after being deported from the United States during the height of the Red Scare. For some time, even when in Russia, both were rather apprehensive about the rumors regarding anarchists being arrested by the Bolshevik government. It wasn't until the Kronstadt uprising that both realized what was taking place. It was at this time that they began to do work with the ABC, which was known during this period as the Society to Aid Anarchists Imprisoned in Russia.—Ed.

12 Tatyana Polosova, a member of the Society to Aid Imprisoned Anarchists, was arrested by the Cheka while she was helping a prisoners' child visit its parent. Both were placed in the Archangel prison. She was later transferred to Poltava, where she was found by the aid organization to be without basic necessities and without work. Lea Gutman and Helena Ganshina, also delegates for the aid organization were sent to travel the north distributing food, clothing, and other vital

necessities among the political prisoners in the prisons and camps of Archangel Province. During their trip to the north, the anarchists in Pertominsky prison declared a hunger strike for better living conditions. Because Gutman, Ganshina, and another comrade informed the others in Petrograd and Moscow about the hunger strike, they were arrested and sent to a Moscow prison. Both Gutman and Ganshina were sentenced to two years in Beresov in the Tobolsk Province. A seven-day hunger strike forced the authorities to change the place of exile. Gutman was transferred and remained in exile in the town of Zinovievsk; Ganshina was transferred from prison to prison and was last known to have been in Siberia.—Ed.

13   Members of the Society to Aid Anarchist Prisoners in Russia were soon arrested and many of them later killed. On July 9, 1923, forty-one anarchists were arrested in the city of Petrograd. The Cheka raided their apartments and placed them under arrest for propagating anarchist ideas, under article 60-63 of the Soviet Criminal Code. Several of those arrested, including Mollie Steimer, Senya Fleshin, and Maria Veger, were arrested for their connections to Goldman and Berkman in Berlin, as well as their prisoner aid work. Due to additional protests by foreign anarcho-syndicalist delegates at the Profintern, Steimer and Fleshin were released and were informed of their impending deportation. On September 27, 1923, both Fleshin and Steimer were placed on a boat headed for Germany. Once in Berlin, the two met up with Berkman, Goldman, Schapiro, Volin, Mratchny, and others, where they continued to do work providing aid to political prisoners in Russia. Veger was transferred from prison to prison before being placed in Archangel.—Ed.

VII REVIVAL OF RELIEF IN THE USA, 1921–39

1   After hearing the call put out by Berkman, Goldman, and Schapiro, the New York chapter of the Political Prisoners' Defense and Relief Committee reorganized itself as the Anarchist Red Cross. The organization changed its exclusive focus on prisoners in the United States to a much broader scope of prisoners on an international level.—Ed.

2   As before, the group began to organize benefit shows to raise money. On November 12, 1924, the Anarchist Red Cross held a benefit show at the Jewish Art Theater at 27th Street and 4th Avenue in New York. Outings and dinners were also organized for the benefit of the political prisoners in Russia. The group in New York, along with the Joint Committee in Berlin, began to make joint pleas, in anarchist and other radical publications, for assistance to aid all revolutionaries imprisoned in Russian jails. *Road to Freedom* 1, no. 1, November 1924; *Road to Freedom* 1, no. 2, December 1924.—Ed.

3   The Workmen's Circle Labor Lyceum was located at 3202 W. Ogden Avenue. Originally called the Douglas Park Auditorium, the Workmen's Circle bought the building in 1923, before changing its name. They used the location to provide medical benefits, burial provisions, and

educational and recreational programs for the larger Jewish community. The location also served as a meeting place for political and labor organizations. Irving Cutler, *Jews of Chicago, From Shtetl to Suburb* (Chicago: University of Illinois Press, 1996), 218.—Ed.

4   The Kropotkin Literary Society, Branch 413, Workmen's Circle, Los Angeles, was one of those organizations who answered the call for support. This branch of the Workmen's Circle comprised anarchists and raised funds by publishing anarchist literature in English. The organization began organizing their own Arestantin Ball. *Freie Arbeiter Stimme*, December 9, 1927; April 19, 1929; March 4, 1932.—Ed.

5   Like in so many other cities, the Libertarian Group in Los Angeles organized Arestantin Balls to raise funds for political prisoners in Russia. Some of these benefits took place at the Folks House at 420 North Soto Street in Los Angeles. Many of those active in the Libertarian Group in Los Angeles had been active in the ARC in other cities before coming to Los Angeles. Bessie Kimmelman, for example, was active in the Cleveland ARC and the Sacco-Vanzetti Defense Committee. She moved to Los Angeles in 1927 and continued her political activity. Mark Mratchny who became active in the Anarchist Black Cross and the Society to Aid Anarchist Prisoners in Russia briefly lived in Los Angeles and participated in the Libertarian Group.—Ed.

6   One of those active in the New York Anarchist Red Cross was the infamous labor leader Rose Pesotta. During the 1922 and 1924 ILGWU conventions, Rose proposed a resolution demanding the liberation of all political prisoners in Russia to a crowd that was not entirely happy about this demand.—Ed.

7   Maximoff died on March 16, 1950.—Ed.

8   Several former members of the Anarchist Red Cross fell victim to these purges, some despite having for years advocated cooperation with the Bolshevik government. Bill Shatov is believed to have been arrested and then shot during the purges. Another former New York ARC member, Efim Yarchuk, who had left Russia in 1922, had a change of heart and appealed for permission to return to Russia. He was allowed to return in 1925. Sadly, Yarchuk disappeared during these purges as well.—Ed.

9   Here it may be well remarked that a change in our status had already taken place in 1932, when, at a special meeting, the Secretariat of the International Working Men's Association Russian Aid Fund in Europe decided that since the Chicago Aid Fund was the most active group in the work of helping prisoners in Russia, the proposition should be made that we become the Chicago Aid Fund Section of the International Working Men's Association. We accepted the title and worked under it for several years.

10   Olay died in April 1943.—Ed.

11   It must be noted that Emma Goldman, who also worked with the Black Cross, also assisted with the SIA. Information about that can be found in most books relating to her life.—Ed.

VIII THE SECOND WORLD WAR

1   Sam Frydman (also spelled Friedman) was a member of the Anarchist
     Red Cross in Chicago and the Union of Russian Workers. In response
     to the Russian Revolution, he traveled to Russia and for a short
     period of time joined Makhno's army. He later moved to Odessa
     where he met his wife, Dora, a fellow anarchist who had been active
     in the Confederation of Anarchist Organizations of Ukraine aka
     "Nabat." While in Odessa, Frydman joined the Odessa Federation of
     Anarchists. In the autumn of 1919, he was arrested in Moscow on
     suspicion of being a member of the Moscow organization Anarchists
     of the Underground. They left Russia in 1923, eventually arriving in
     Paris, where they became active in a Jewish group as well as the Relief
     Fund of the International Workers' Association for Imprisoned and
     Exiled Anarchists and Anarcho-Syndicalists in Russia. Sam and Dora
     had a daughter, Michelle. However, in 1942, after the German inva-
     sion, Frydman and his wife were arrested by Nazi soldiers and sent to
     Auschwitz. Michelle was saved thanks to comrades who hid her. Sam
     and Dora were not heard from again. *Kate Sharpley Bulletin*, no. 74–75
     (August 2013): 11.—Ed.

2   He [Baruch Charney Vladeck] died on October 31, 1938.

3   Mollie Steimer and her partner, Senya Fleshin, being Jewish anar-
     chists and now living in Paris soon found themselves facing the fear of
     arrests and death at the hands of Nazis. On May 18, 1940, Steimer was
     placed in a Nazi internment camp. Aided by French comrades, Senya
     was able to escape from the Nazis to an unoccupied section in France.
     Miraculously, Mollie Steimer was able to secure her release and was
     able to meet up with Volin and Fleshin in Marseilles in 1941. She and
     Fleshin later fled to Mexico.—Ed.

IX POSTWAR ACTIVITIES, 1945

1   As an appendix I am printing an article by B. Axler, secretary of the
     Jewish Anarchist Federation, dealing with the 25th anniversary of the
     Alexander Berkman Aid Fund.

X CONSERVATISM AND FACTIONALISM

1   I knew when I started to prepare this book that many of our Jewish
     comrades who are still taking part, for one reason or another, in the
     work of the Jewish Labor Committee would not be pleased by my bring-
     ing up this question. Recently a few of them approached me about it
     and in one particular incident came to me with the argument that the
     Jewish Labor Committee did in fact help our comrades. To this friend,
     I would say that I know about the "help" in question, and later on I will
     give the relevant figures. At present, however, I want to remark that
     what the JLC gave was no more than a sop to allay the growing volume
     of protest at its partisanship. This view was held by others than me,
     and in support of it I quote a letter from Alexander Schapiro, written

in reply to a request of mine that he should represent the Alexander Berkman Aid Fund in an attempt to get some help from the JLC. "No matter who your representative may be," he said, "I can assure you that you will get from the Jewish Labor Committee something in the form of a bribe. I personally will not take part in this matter under any circumstances."

APPENDIX 2

1   Paul Avrich, *The Modern School Movement* (Oakland: AK Press, 2002), 216–17.

2   "Murphy Flees Fearing Frame-Up," *New York Times*, July 7, 1914, 20.

3   Avrich, *Modern School Movement*, 216; *Mother Earth* 9, no. 5, July 1914, 156–57.

4   Avrich, *Modern School Movement*, 216; *Mother Earth* 9, no. 5, July 1914, 157–58.

5   Avrich, *Modern School Movement*, 216; *Mother Earth* 9, no. 5, July 1914, 156–57.

6   Paul Avrich, *Anarchist Voices* (Princeton: Princeton University Press, 1995), 110.

7   Avrich. *Anarchist Voices*, 124.

8   Paul Avrich, *Sacco and Vanzetti: The Anarchist Background* (Princeton: Princeton University Press, 1991), 100.

9   Avrich *Anarchist Voices*, 125.

10 Avrich. *Sacco and Vanzetti*, 100.

11 "Find Berg's Body in Wreckage," *New York Times*, July 6, 1914; Joseph Cohen, *The Jewish Anarchist Movement in America* (Chico: AK Press, 2024) 347–49.

12 "Find Berg's Body in Wreckage," *New York Times*, July 6, 1914.

13 "Exploded in Apartment Occupied by Tarryton Disturbers," *New York Times*. July 5, 1914.

14 Avrich, *Modern School Movement*, 203; Cohen, *Jewish Anarchist Movement*, 347–49.

15 Avrich, *Anarchist Voices*, 389.

16 Avrich, *Anarchist Voices*, 110.

17 Adolf Wolff, "To Our Martyred Dead," *Mother Earth* 9, no. 5 (July 1914).

18 "Can't Talk Over Bomb Men's Bodies," *New York Times*, July 8, 1914.

19 "Bodies of the Dead Anarchists Burned," *New York Times*, July 9, 1914.

20 Emma Goldman, *Living My Life* (Garden City: Garden City Publishing, 1934), 537.

21 "5000 at Memorial to Anarchist Dead," *New York Times*. July 12, 1914.

22 "Lexington Explosion," *Mother Earth* 9, no. 5 (July 1914): 155.

23 Francis M. Naumann; Paul Avrich, "Adolf Wolff: Poet, Sculptor and Revolutionist, but Mostly Revolutionist," *Art Bulletin* 67, no. 3 (September 1985): 495–96.

24 Avrich, *Anarchist Voices*, 207.

25 Goldman. *Living My Life*, 537.

26 "Francis Menaced by Anarchists," *New York Times*, January 31, 1918; Goldman. *Living My Life,* 638.

27 FBI, Old German Files, 1909–21, Louise Berger (#8000-364032).

28 "Police Close to Bomb Plot Perpetrator," *New York Tribune*, June 7, 1919; Avrich. *Anarchist Voices,* 389.

INDEX

Page numbers in *italic* refer to illustrations. "Passim" (literally "scattered") indicates intermittent discussion of a topic over a cluster of pages.

ABOUT THE CONTRIBUTORS

Boris Yelensky (1889–1974) was a Russian anarchist propagandist who took part in the 1905 Russian Revolution. Due to czarist repression, he was forced to flee the country in 1907, eventually landing in the US. He helped to establish the Philadelphia and Chicago chapters of the Anarchist Red Cross. Yelensky later returned to Russia to participate in the 1917 Revolution. With Lenin's rise to power and the increased repression against anarchists, Yelensky once again left his native country, settling permanently in the US. Once he returned to the US, he continued to provide support for imprisoned anarchists through his work in the Alexander Berkman Aid Fund, a section of the Anarchist Red Cross. For over fifty years he was an important figure in Chicago's Free Society Group and active in the Anarchist Red Cross.

Matthew Hart is an educator and labor activist from the greater Los Angeles area. His participation in the political movement began with Whittier Food Not Bombs and the antiglobalization movement in the mid-1990s. In 1998, he helped to establish the Los Angeles chapter of the Anarchist Black Cross. Throughout the years, he has engaged in extensive research and archiving of the Anarchist Black Cross history. Hart has spent several decades in the labor movement as a rank-and-file activist and staff and teaches labor studies courses at Los Angeles Trade Technical College.

N.O. Bonzo is an anarchist illustrator, printmaker, and muralist based in Portland, OR. They are the illustrator of *Mutual Aid: An Illuminated Factor of Evolution* and creator of *Off with Their Heads: An Antifascist Coloring Book for Adults of All Ages*; *Beneath the Pavement the Garden: An Anarchist Coloring Book for All Ages*; and *The Beautiful Idea.*

ABOUT PM PRESS

PM Press is an independent, radical publisher of critically necessary books for our tumultuous times. Our aim is to deliver bold political ideas and vital stories to all walks of life and arm the dreamers to demand the impossible. Founded in 2007 by a small group of people with decades of publishing, media, and organizing experience, we have sold millions of copies of our books, most often one at a time, face to face. We're old enough to know what we're doing and young enough to know what's at stake. Join us to create a better world.

PM Press
PO Box 23912
Oakland, CA 94623
www.pmpress.org

PM Press in Europe
europe@pmpress.org
www.pmpress.org.uk

FRIENDS OF PM PRESS

These are indisputably momentous times—the financial system is melting down globally and the Empire is stumbling. Now more than ever there is a vital need for radical ideas.

In the many years since its founding—and on a mere shoestring—PM Press has risen to the formidable challenge of publishing and distributing knowledge and entertainment for the struggles ahead. With hundreds of releases to date, we have published an impressive and stimulating array of literature, art, music, politics, and culture. Using every available medium, we've succeeded in connecting those hungry for ideas and information to those putting them into practice.

Friends of PM allows you to directly help impact, amplify, and revitalize the discourse and actions of radical writers, filmmakers, and artists. It provides us with a stable foundation from which we can build upon our early successes and provides a much-needed subsidy for the materials that can't necessarily pay their own way. You can help make that happen—and receive every new title automatically delivered to your door once a month—by joining as a Friend of PM Press. And, we'll throw in a free T-shirt when you sign up.

Here are your options:

- **$30 a month** Get all books and pamphlets plus a 50% discount on all webstore purchases

- **$40 a month** Get all PM Press releases (including CDs and DVDs) plus a 50% discount on all webstore purchases

- **$100 a month** Superstar—Everything plus PM merchandise, free downloads, and a 50% discount on all webstore purchases

For those who can't afford $30 or more a month, we have **Sustainer Rates** at $15, $10 and $5. Sustainers get a free PM Press T-shirt and a 50% discount on all purchases from our website.

Your Visa or Mastercard will be billed once a month, until you tell us to stop. Or until our efforts succeed in bringing the revolution around. Or the financial meltdown of Capital makes plastic redundant. Whichever comes first.

No Harmless Power: The Life and Times of the Ukrainian Anarchist Nestor Makhno

Charlie Allison
Illustrated by Kevin Matthews and N.O. Bonzo

ISBN: 978-1-62963-471-5
$21.95   256 pages

Lively, incendiary, and inspiring, *No Harmless Power* follows the life of Nestor Makhno, who organized a seven-million-strong anarchist polity during the Russian Civil War and developed Platformist anarchism during his exile in Paris as well as advising other anarchists like Durruti on tactics and propaganda. Both timely and timeless, this biography reveals Makhno's rapidly changing world and his place in it. He moved swiftly from peasant youth to prisoner to revolutionary anarchist leader, narrowly escaping Bolshevik Ukraine for Paris. This book also chronicles the friends and enemies he made along the way: Lenin, Trotsky, Kropotkin, Alexander Berkman, Emma Goldman, Ida Mett, and others.

No Harmless Power is the first text to fully delve into Makhno's sympathy for the downtrodden, the trap of personal heroism, his improbable victories, unlikely friendships, and his alarming lack of gun safety in meetings. Makhno and the movement he began are seldom mentioned in most mainstream histories—Western or Russian—mostly on the grounds that acknowledging anarchist polities calls into question the inevitability and desirability of the nation-state and unjust hierarchies.

With illustrations by N.O. Bonzo and Kevin Matthews, this is a fresh, humorous, and necessary look at an under examined corner of history as well as a deep exploration of the meaning—and value, if any—of heroism as history.

"A biography that reads like a great adventure story, this tale of freedom-fighting and myth-making in early-twentieth-century Eastern Europe is as entertaining as it is necessary."
—Stephanie Feldman, author of *Angel of Losses* and *Saturnalia*

Mutual Aid: An Illuminated Factor of Evolution

Peter Kropotkin
Illustrated by N.O. Bonzo with an Introduction by David Graeber & Andrej Grubačić, Foreword by Ruth Kinna, Postscript by GATS, and an Afterword by Allan Antliff

ISBN: 978-1-62963-874-4 (paperback)
978-1-62963-875-1 (hardcover)
$30.00/$59.95   336 pages

One hundred years after his death, Peter Kropotkin is still one of the most inspirational figures of the anarchist movement. It is often forgotten that Kropotkin was also a world-renowned geographer whose seminal critique of the hypothesis of competition promoted by social Darwinism helped revolutionize modern evolutionary theory. An admirer of Darwin, he used his observations of life in Siberia as the basis for his 1902 collection of essays *Mutual Aid: A Factor of Evolution*. Kropotkin demonstrated that mutually beneficial cooperation and reciprocity—in both individuals and as a species—plays a far more important role in the animal kingdom and human societies than does individualized competitive struggle. Kropotkin carefully crafted his theory making the science accessible. His account of nature rejected Rousseau's romantic depictions and ethical socialist ideas that cooperation was motivated by the notion of "universal love." His understanding of the dynamics of social evolution shows us the power of cooperation—whether it is bison defending themselves against a predator or workers unionizing against their boss. His message is clear: solidarity is strength!

Every page of this new edition of *Mutual Aid* has been beautifully illustrated by one of anarchism's most celebrated current artists, N.O. Bonzo. The reader will also enjoy original artwork by GATS and insightful commentary by David Graeber, Ruth Kinna, Andrej Grubačić, and Allan Antliff.

Anarchy and the Sex Question: Essays on Women and Emancipation, 1896–1926

Emma Goldman
Edited by Shawn P. Wilbur

ISBN: 978-1-62963-144-8
$14.95   160 pages

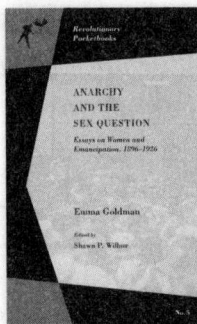

For Emma Goldman, the "High Priestess of Anarchy," anarchism was "a living force in the affairs of our life, constantly creating new conditions," but "the most elemental force in human life" was something still more basic and vital: sex.

"The Sex Question" emerged for Goldman in multiple contexts, and we find her addressing it in writing on subjects as varied as women's suffrage, "free love," birth control, the "New Woman," homosexuality, marriage, love, and literature. It was at once a political question, an economic question, a question of morality, and a question of social relations.

But her analysis of that most elemental force remained fragmentary, scattered across numerous published (and unpublished) works and conditioned by numerous contexts. *Anarchy and the Sex Question* draws together the most important of those scattered sources, uniting both familiar essays and archival material, in an attempt to recreate the great work on sex that Emma Goldman might have given us. In the process, it sheds light on Goldman's place in the history of feminism.

"Emma Goldman left a profound legacy of wisdom, insight, and passionate commitment to life. Shawn Wilbur has carefully selected her best writings on that most profound, pleasurable, and challenging of topics: sex. This collection is a great service to anarchist, feminist, and queer communities around the world."
—Jamie Heckert, coeditor of *Anarchism & Sexuality: Ethics, Relationships and Power*

"Shawn Wilbur has done a great job assembling and introducing Emma Goldman's writings on women, feminism, and sexuality. As he notes, Goldman's essays continue to provoke and inspire. The collection artfully documents the evolution of Goldman's views on freedom, sex, and human liberation."
—Robert Graham, editor of *Anarchism: A Documentary History of Libertarian Ideas*

Words of a Rebel

Peter Kropotkin
Translated and edited by Iain
McKay
with a Preface by Elisée Reclus

ISBN: 978-1-62963-877-5
$24.95   320 pages

Peter Kropotkin remains one of the best-
known anarchist thinkers, and *Words of a Rebel*
was his first libertarian book. Published in
1885 while he was in a French jail for anarchist activism, this collection
of articles from the newspaper *Le Revolté* sees Kropotkin criticise the
failings of capitalism and those who seek to end it by means of its main
support, the state. Instead, he urged the creation of a mass movement
from below that would expropriate property and destroy the state,
replacing their centralised hierarchies with federations of self-governing
communities and workplaces.

Kropotkin's instant classic included discussions themes and ideas
he returned to repeatedly during his five decades in the anarchist
movement. Unsurprisingly, *Words of a Rebel* was soon translated into
numerous languages—including Italian, Spanish, Bulgarian, Russian, and
Chinese—and reprinted time and time again. But despite its influence
as Kropotkin's first anarchist work, it was the last to be completely
translated into English.

This is a new translation from the French original by Iain McKay except
for a few chapters previously translated by Nicolas Walter. Both
anarchist activists and writers, they are well placed to understand
the assumptions within and influences on Kropotkin's revolutionary
journalism. It includes all the original 1885 text along with the preface to
the 1904 Italian as well as the preface and afterward to the 1919 Russian
editions. In addition, it includes many articles on the labour movement
written by Kropotkin for *Le Revolté* which show how he envisioned
getting from criticism to a social revolution. Along with a comprehensive
glossary and an introduction by Iain McKay placing this work within the
history of anarchism as well as indicating its relevance to radicals and
revolutionaries today, this is the definitive edition of an anarchist classic.

Anarchy, Geography, Modernity: Selected Writings of Elisée Reclus

Edited by John P. Clark and
Camille Martin

ISBN: 978-1-60486-429-8
$22.95   304 pages

Anarchy, Geography, Modernity is the first
comprehensive introduction to the thought
of Elisée Reclus, the great anarchist geographer and political theorist.
It shows him to be an extraordinary figure for his age. Not only an
anarchist but also a radical feminist, anti-racist, ecologist, animal rights
advocate, cultural radical, nudist, and vegetarian. Not only a major social
thinker but also a dedicated revolutionary.

The work analyzes Reclus' greatest achievement, a sweeping historical
and theoretical synthesis recounting the story of the earth and
humanity as an epochal struggle between freedom and domination. It
presents his groundbreaking critique of all forms of domination: not
only capitalism, the state, and authoritarian religion, but also patriarchy,
racism, technological domination, and the domination of nature. His
crucial insights on the interrelation between personal and small-
group transformation, broader cultural change, and large-scale social
organization are explored. Reclus' ideas are presented both through
detailed exposition and analysis, and in extensive translations of key
texts, most appearing in English for the first time.

*"For far too long Elisée Reclus has stood in the shadow of Godwin, Proudhon,
Bakunin, Kropotkin, and Emma Goldman. Now John Clark has pulled Reclus
forward to stand shoulder to shoulder with Anarchism's cynosures. Reclus'
light brought into anarchism's compass not only a focus on ecology, but a
struggle against both patriarchy and racism, contributions which can now
be fully appreciated thanks to John Clark's exegesis and [his and Camille
Martin's] translations of works previously unavailable in English. No serious
reader can afford to neglect this book."*
—Dana Ward, Pitzer College

*"Finally! A century after his death, the great French geographer and anarchist
Elisée Reclus has been honored by a vibrant selection of his writings expertly
translated into English."*
—Kent Mathewson, Louisiana State University

A Soldier's Story: Revolutionary Writings by a New Afrikan Anarchist, Third Edition

Kuwasi Balagoon, edited by Matt Meyer and Karl Kersplebedeb

ISBN: 978-1-62963-377-0
$19.95   272 pages

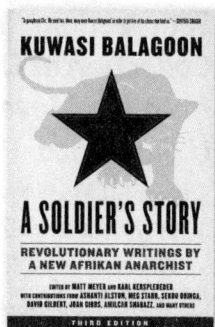

Kuwasi Balagoon was a participant in the Black Liberation struggle from the 1960s until his death in prison in 1986. A member of the Black Panther Party and defendant in the infamous Panther 21 case, Balagoon went underground with the Black Liberation Army (BLA). Captured and convicted of various crimes against the state, he spent much of the 1970s in prison, escaping twice. After each escape, he went underground and resumed BLA activity.

Balagoon was unusual for his time in several ways. He combined anarchism with Black nationalism, he broke the rules of sexual and political conformity that surrounded him, he took up arms against the white-supremacist state—all the while never shying away from developing his own criticisms of the weaknesses within the movements. His eloquent trial statements and political writings, as much as his poetry and excerpts from his prison letters, are all testimony to a sharp and iconoclastic revolutionary who was willing to make hard choices and fully accept the consequences.

Balagoon was captured for the last time in December 1981, charged with participating in an armored truck expropriation in West Nyack, New York, an action in which two police officers and a money courier were killed. Convicted and sentenced to life imprisonment, he died of an AIDS-related illness on December 13, 1986.

The first part of this book consists of contributions by those who knew or were touched by Balagoon. The second section consists of court statements and essays by Balagoon himself, including several documents that were absent from previous editions and have never been published before. The third consists of excerpts from letters Balagoon wrote from prison. A final fourth section consists of a historical essay by Akinyele Umoja and an extensive intergenerational roundtable discussion of the significance of Balagoon's life and thoughts today.

Let Freedom Ring: A Collection of Documents from the Movements to Free U.S. Political Prisoners

Edited by Matt Meyer with afterwords by Ashanti Alston and Lynne Stewart

ISBN: 978-1-60486-035-1
$37.95   912 pages

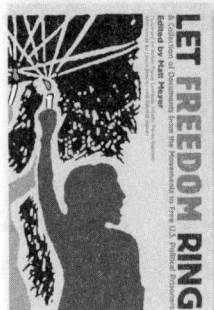

Let Freedom Ring presents a two-decade sweep of essays, analyses, histories, interviews, resolutions, People's Tribunal verdicts, and poems by and about the scores of U.S. political prisoners and the campaigns to safeguard their rights and secure their freedom. In addition to an extensive section on the campaign to free death-row journalist Mumia Abu-Jamal, represented here are the radical movements that have most challenged the U.S. empire from within: Black Panthers and other Black liberation fighters, Puerto Rican independentistas, Indigenous sovereignty activists, white anti-imperialists, environmental and animal rights militants, Arab and Muslim activists, Iraq war resisters, and others. Contributors in and out of prison detail the repressive methods—from long-term isolation to sensory deprivation to politically inspired parole denial—used to attack these freedom fighters, some still caged after 30+ years. This invaluable resource guide offers inspiring stories of the creative, and sometimes winning, strategies to bring them home.

Contributors include: Mumia Abu-Jamal, Dan Berger, Dhoruba Bin-Wahad, Bob Lederer, Terry Bisson, Laura Whitehorn, Safiya Bukhari, The San Francisco 8, Angela Davis, Bo Brown, Bill Dunne, Jalil Muntaqim, Susie Day, Luis Nieves Falcón, Ninotchka Rosca, Meg Starr, Assata Shakur, Jill Soffiyah Elijah, Jan Susler, Chrystos, Jose Lopez, Leonard Peltier, Marilyn Buck, Oscar López Rivera, Sundiata Acoli, Ramona Africa, Linda Thurston, Desmond Tutu, Mairead Corrigan Maguire and many more.

"Within every society there are people who, at great personal risk and sacrifice, stand up and fight for the most marginalized among us. We call these people of courage, spirit and love, our heroes and heroines. This book is the story of the ones in our midst. It is the story of the best we are."
— asha bandele, poet and author of *The Prisoner's Wife*